GW00392740

Journey Without Plans (or Ideas)
Another Romanian Adventure

Gary & Helen Bacon

"Once you have travelled, the voyage never ends, but is played out over and over again in the quietest chambers. The mind can never break off from the journey."

Pat Conroy

This book, such as it is, is dedicated to the people who have given us wanderlust ("A very strong or irresistible impulse to travel"). These include Gary's maternal grandfather, C W Stenton, who despite his age, professional and marital status (which exempted him from service in the Second World War) enlisted because he wanted *to see the world*. Much of where he went and what he did are lost in the annals of history, we know that he spent time in North Africa and Burma (where he was mentioned in despatches contracted malaria, that would eventually kill him) but beyond that we know very little.

The second are our parents; Gary's who in the mid-1950s decided to have a holiday touring parts of Western Europe by motorbike and showed me that money should not be a barrier to travel (although it may limit how much cheese you can afford!) and Helen's who, well into their eighties have continued to travel and explore with their touring caravan.

Contents

Gary, as always, writing the journal which is reproduced here.

Helen planning our next move.

Acknowledgments

"Writing is its own reward." **Henry Miller**

The last book was born out of a desire to firstly write a book and secondly fulfil a promise to a man on a plane that told me I should write up my diary. Initially as I was writing it I found it quite an onerous task as I tried to work out what some of the words were and the context in which they were written, such is my awful handwriting. But when I finished it I did feel spiritually rewarded. It was not a way to fame and fortune (it was never meant to be) and I'm sure that if I worked out how much it cost me in time then I would find that any breakeven point is a long way in the future.

So, if this is true and it was such a chore then why dear reader are you sitting there about to trawl through another seventy plus thousand words. Umberto Eco (in The Island of the Day Before) said,, "To survive, you must tell stories" and as someone who loves oral history and oratory in general it is a rather cathartic process to sit down and type up the rough notes from our adventures in Romania.

Now to the problem of acknowledgements. After the last book I had a few emails/conversations from people asking if they were mentioned and they seem disappointed when they weren't. Sorry about that. The reason is, as with Oscar speeches, if I'm not careful then the thanks will go on and on in every book. So, if I've missed you out (again) then I'm sorry.

KLM were, once more wonderful in getting us to and from Romania and Tarom flew us internally up to the wonderfully local (small) 'international' airport in Iasi, both very smooth and highly recommended airlines.

Bookings.com, Airbnb and RailPlanner all made our travelling easier as, due to the power of the internet, we could sort out accommodation as and when required. Without these apps, we would have had to plan properly rather than as you will see, wing it more than was really necessary. Gone are the days when you had to carry around a copy of the Thomas Cook International Railway Timetable in order catch a train and much of the mystique has gone with it.

To thank a whole school might seem a little excessive, but both of our Romanian adventures were bookended by my teaching at Horizon Community College in Barnsley and the support given to me by staff and pupils was wonderful. This was especially true when the first book was released and several pupils thought that I was going to be as rich as J K Rowling.

In the Acknowledgements for "Travels With…" I listed many of the authors whose work I have read over the years and I'm not going to do that again. The one who I must thank is the late Graham Greene whose titles have influenced my choice greatly and I would recommend both Travels With My Aunt and Journey Without Maps, without question, they are much better books than this!

Helen has had much more influence on this book than the last one and so gets special thanks for putting her oar in in the right place and making sure that I didn't put anything in that could be deemed as libellous (or just wrong).

Finally you will notice that the narrative changes at times between I and we. I wish I could say that this is deliberate in order to create a joint narrative. It's not, it's down to sloppy writing. Sorry.

A Map!

A brief overview of what we did (for those of you who don't want to read the whole thing......and who can blame you!).

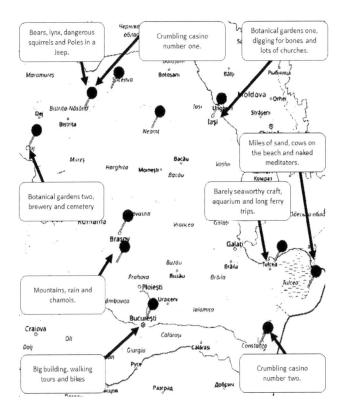

MONDAY	TUESDAY	WEDNESDAY	THURSDAY	FRIDAY	SATURDAY	SUNDAY
31	1 — IASI — LAVRA BISTRO INN	2 — IASI LAVRA BISTRA BOTANICAL GARDEN	3 — IASI — LAVRA AGAPO	4 — RADNA NEAMT MUSEUMS	5 — PIATRA NEAMT CAVE CAL	6 — PIATRA NSAMT — CUGA —
7 — KLUNA MONASTERIES	8 —	9 — VATRA DORNEI	10 — VATRA DORNEI ← ULQ CAMP →	11 — VATRA DORNA —	12 — CLUS —	13 — CLUS —
14 — 15 CLUS — BRASOV —	15	16 —	17 BUSTEAMI	18 —	19 ← DOBRU — TULCEA	20 — ← STG
21 — STG	22 —	23 —	24 — CONSTANTA	25 —	26 — ONCE HOTEL — BUCHAREST →	27 — BUCHAREST —
28 BUCHAREST —	29 BUCHAREST →	30	31			

The closest we got to a plan is this grid that slowly filled up as the trip progressed. An omission was the overnight stop that we were forced to do in Bucharest on 17th August because of train times (due to a cancelled train). By keeping this grid, we were aware of how long we had before we had to get somewhere and from the midpoint of the trip it gave us times and places to target. This was mainly Bucharest at the end where we had accommodation booked.

The Start

So, here we were again. Another holiday that we hoped would turn into an adventure, but, why Romania again? That, dear reader, is an excellent question considering that this was our fourth visit to the country in a little over two years (two with the Scouts and two on our own).

Just before we left for our 2017 adventure I finally delivered what was hopefully the final draft of the 2016 trip to Margaret Thoms, a good friend of ours, who had agreed to edit and correct the awful English before I could get 'Travels With My Wife' published[1]. This meant that I was going to be living the sequel whilst the original was still being mulled over.[2]

Oh yes, Romania, why there again? Well, it offers a fascinating challenge for any independent traveller. The sort of person who has the right attitude when things go wrong, does not get frustrated and is happy to struggle to get anywhere and seeing this as part of the adventure. If you have the ability to sit back and let problems wash over you, then you will love the country. Some trains will break down and bits will fall off the wall in hotels without warning, but that's half the fun. I'm sure that many Eastern European, ex-Communist countries are similar, but travelling in them is fun if you do it right, accept that there might be problems and as H always says, "Roll with it".

---

[1] At the time of passing on the manuscript I had no idea what I was going to do with it once it was done other than it was going to be a book!
2 It would not be until the summer of 2018 that Travels was finally published through the good people at Kindle Direct Publishing.

When we were dropped off at the airport to head home after our previous trip the taxi driver promised that he would look after the country for us while we were away. Whilst we accept that change is inevitable the spread of the McDonalds/Starbucks flags appears to stifle local competition – we hope that its move through Romania has slowed.

In 2016 we had tried to head towards the Ukraine border, to the north of the country, using only public transport. Sadly we established that this was not possible without risking getting stuck and that trying to cross from west to east, from where we had reached, could not be done due to the Borsec Gap[3]. So our plan for 2017 was to initially explore the north east of the country beyond Iasi and fill in what Shipton called, "The Blanks on the Map"[4]. This involved an internal flight up to Iasi in the north east towards the Moldavian Border and then trying to head west. Our thought was that travelling this way would take us, eventually, into known territory.

---

[3] This was our name for a stretch of road about 30 miles long near the town of Borsec where, try as we might, we could not get across by public transport.

[4] Blank on the Map: 'Pioneering Exploration of the Shaksgam Valley and Karakoram Mountains' by Eric Shipton. It is written about an expedition he did in 1937 and has the wonderful quote of 'As I studied the maps, one thing about them captured my imagination ... across this blank space was written one challenging word, 'Unexplored' – we were filling in our own blanks.

Week One

And so, another adventure begins.

To set the scene, on Sunday 30th July H's nephew got married and so we spent the day attending the wedding, the reception etc. We did leave at a reasonable hour (10pm) but after we checked and rechecked our passports, currency, rucsacs and passports again, it was a little after 11pm by the time we finally went to bed. It was just as well that we didn't put sleep as a high priority as we didn't really get any.

Monday 31st July – We have an earlier flight than 2016 and so adjust our times accordingly. This means that the taxi is booked for 1am. After a sort of nap the alarm goes off. A cup of tea later and we are standing outside waiting for the taxi (the house key stowed in the top of H's rucsac, the now standard storage place where we hope we will find it in four weeks time).

I'm not sure if it's ironic but we are picked up by a VW Jetta, similar to the car that we had hired in Romania last year (one that was far bigger than we required, caused me nightmares and H to laugh as I crashed the gears a lot). Our rucsacs are easily stowed away in the cavernous boot (we knew they would be) and off we set.

This year our choice of company is City Taxis and we have a lovely driver who is normally a cook in the family restaurant. His reasons for spending his summer holidays driving a taxi is not fully disclosed, but he is good company and we happily chat with him before we finally get on the Woodhead Pass (his satnav takes us a very odd way to the motorway) and we both fall asleep.

On the other side of the Pennines I realise that we are going to be way too early at the airport. Dropped off at Terminal Three where our driver admits that he has a fear of flying and snakes.

We go to check in to find that ours is the second flight out this morning, after one to Lanzarote (we fly at 5.55). Due to the early hour nothing is open, no check-in desks or anything. Last year we were on a flight two hours later so at least some things were open. I sit down and read my Kindle whilst H takes a much more practical approach, getting her sleeping mat out and trying to get some sleep[5].

The airport slowly fills up and people start to queue even though none of the desks are open or showing any signs of life. Many have discovered that by using the airlines scales you can save a pound and are trying to do it without anyone seeing, even though a long queue has formed of people who want to do the same.

After some debate we join the queue and are impressed with how quickly it is moving. Sadly, as we are almost at the desk the bloke in front of us finds that his bag weighs 26+ kgs and so is forced to repack. This he does at the front of the queue rather than just stepping to one side and letting other people book in. The check in assistant sighs as does everyone else in the queue sigh. By comparison our rucsacs are lightweights with H's coming in at 12kg and mine at 13kg.

---

[5] She has limited success.

The Osprey rucsac covers[6] that we are using make our luggage look like body bags as we drag them over to the non-standard luggage area that we are directed to, again, with the instruction, "It's under the zebra"[7]. Due to our early arrival we quickly clear the X-ray machine with the only real oddity being the operator asking us if we have any hair straighteners (we obviously don't yet look like wizened travellers).

We go through into the departure area and find a Costa Coffee, it looks like it's going to be a long day so we might as well get started early. H has a breakfast porridge. I show my card and then realise that we appear to be paying normal prices rather than being charged an airport 'supplement', could this be the shape of bargains to come?

Called through to Gate 53 at about 5.05am but, as we have come to expect, that doesn't mean that we can start boarding at that time. It just means that we can go and queue somewhere else. Business Class and Fast Trackers load first then the rest of us. Why there has to be a mass surge to be first on the plane still amazes me. I'm pretty sure that we all have a seat reserved. Through this organised chaos I hear a voice shout "Mr Bacon!" The caller is Lucy Galvin[8] who Gary worked with and is on her way to Australia. We had seen her a couple of days before at a wedding, but we never put two and two together to realise we were both going on the same

---

[6] These are large bags that ensure that rucsac straps etc. are not pulled off as they go through the various bits of machinery at the airport.
[7] A reference to the advertisement that is directly above it. Sadly I did not make a note of what it was advertising, nor can I remember it.
[8] Who we spot due to her recently dyed pink hair.

flight to Amsterdam. A hurried conversation ensues and exchange of hugs before she sets off on a much longer journey than our own.

Once all of the self loading cargo[9] is on board we set off at 6.10 on the short hop to Amsterdam, delayed by 15 minutes due to there being 'a lot of traffic', obviously Manchester airspace rush hour!

By 6.30 we have the food slickly handed out (cheese sandwich, Punselie's Stroopkoekjes biscuit plus water and tea) as it always is on KLM. Then it's time to get some sleep but the noise of the engines drowns out the soothing music on the iPod, wonder if it is the headphones that are a little ropey? Make a mental note to check them when I can access my luggage in the hold where I have spares.

Land in Amsterdam ahead of schedule as the driver had obviously put their foot down (once they were clear of the traffic) and whilst we don't have the long wait we had in 2016 we do have time for a leisurely stroll through to Gate D24. We know which gate as we have both received texts from the airline confirming where we should be going, as if they are tracking us (maybe they are?). Unlike 2016 the gate is relatively close to where we have entered the airport and, whilst we do not have time to shop at the Big Orange Shop, we do have time to do some people watching.

9am and we started trying to load. I say trying as it seems to involve most of the passengers just trying to push their way through (although it is unclear to where!). Everything

---

[9] A phrase from Cabin Pressure by John Finnemore.

grinds to a halt and it takes the intervention of a member of staff (standing in the middle and directing people) for the queues to be sorted and people to start moving forward again. The reason for some of this pushing and shoving soon becomes obvious when an announcement is made (followed by a sign appearing) stating that some hand luggage will have to go in the hold. We don't mind this as our hand luggage is so small that we know that it will be allowed onboard but others have a look of blind panic at the very thought of being separated from their flight bags. Finally, we get up from our seats, book in and walk through to the plane[10].

Even though we are almost the last to board there is still a long delay as baggage is moved around as the KLM staff do a wonderful job repositioning everybody and everything.

H gets a window seat over the wing so she can happily watch the world go around and try and work out where we are. The next three quarters of an hour passes with me being awake (at the start of the safety talk), then asleep (at the end of the safety talk), then awake (for take off) then asleep (whilst climbing to altitude). Finally I am awake as my omelette sandwich arrives. Next to me is a rather ill looking girl who snuggles down on the drop-down table and falls asleep (I am reminded of the infected terrorist in The Cassandra Crossing[11] and decide I should try and hold my breath for the entire trip).

Turbulence and the seatbelt lights come on. I ramble onto H about Clare being sick in New Zealand when we had "real"

---

[10] Remember folks that it's unlikely that they are going to fly off without you so let the queue go down and then get on.

[11] A 1970s disaster film best watched on a rainy Sunday afternoon with a big mug of tea.

turbulence and the plane almost fell out of the sky. The ill girl next to me doesn't budge (she even misses her food). Whilst I am not particularly bothered about the turbulence what does surprise me is the lack of noisy children, where are they all? There were a few at the back of the Amsterdam flight but we could hardly hear them and now there is quiet.

We approach Bucharest from the north and H is sure that we pass over Sibiu (although she doesn't spot the Transfagaras Highway) and wishes that the map was not in the hold so she could try and track our progress. What we do see are lots of almost medieval field systems. Soon we are approaching Bucharest where our landing appears to involve a lot of last minute braking and we are not treated to the softest landing we have had. After saying that it wasn't the worst landing that we have had and we are sure that they will be able to reuse the plane.

Bucharest was once described as the Paris of the East. Whoever said that obviously had never been to the airport. The word practical and utilitarian could have been invented to describe it. Sadly we are not given the chance to walk across the tarmac and, instead, dock with the terminal building using the giant umblical. Queue at passport control passes quicker when we spot some Scouts and try and guess what their nationality is (Belgian?), unfortunately they are too far away for us to ask them or, even more intriguing, find out why one of their party is on crutches (on the way out or the way back?).

So we are back in Bucharest. It doesn't seem to have changed so the taxi driver who I spoke to as we left last year kept his promise[12].

Next question is how do you kill three hours in an airport? Our original plan was to "dash" into Bucharest by taxi but that was a high risk plan that could result in us missing our plane (or being killed by a mad taxi driver). The new plan involved buying some Lavazza Coffee from the café, logging into the free wifi and catching up on emails. We also thought that consulting the Rough Guide might be a good idea as well. The café is decorated with some quite odd, but very artily done, posters. A little research and we find out that they are from their calendars over the years (my favourite is a balancing spoon one from 2003 by Jean-Baptiste Mondino), they certainly make the place look more like a café than part of an airport[13].

Coffee drunk and fearing that we may be overstaying our café time (how long is acceptable to stay in a café having bought one drink?[14]) we set off to try and find where our connecting flight is going from. The logical place to ask, at the TAMRON desk, only results in a general wave in a vague direction from the assistant towards a sign saying "check in". I leave H with the rucsacs and set off in search of a sign for Domestic Departures, there are very few, but lots for International Departures. I finally find it cowering in the corner apparently feeling that its position (below International) means that it doesn't want to make a big deal

---

[12] When I said farewell to the taxi driver who ran us out to the airport after our last trip I told him to make sure that he looked after the country until we returned and he agreed!

[13] https://www.lavazza.co.uk/en/lavazza-world/calendar.html has the full range.

[14] A question that most budget travellers ask....a lot.

about it. Now to just locate where we have to check in before joining the departure queue!

Over the past few years we have established a few things about Romania and what they are good (and not so good) at. What they are most certainly not backwards about coming forwards with is different types of technology, and how it can be used to make life easier. Step forward the Henri Coanda Airport App. Having seen a poster for it I get it and logon using my Facebook details, as these are linked to my KLM account then it picks up the flight for Iasi and tells us exactly where to go.

Zone A is tucked away amongst the 'places you only have to go to if you must' area but we find it and then Desk 02. It is late afternoon and this non-air conditioned part of the airport is rapidly turning into a slow cooker. It's obviously getting to all the staff and, whilst she manages a smile, the assistant dealing with us has the look of someone who wants to jump, fully dressed, into a cold bath screaming "IT'S TOO HOT!!!". We smile politely and put the rucsac's body bags on the scales. Mine, oddly, weighs slightly more despite it not having been opened at all since Manchester!

With our bags on the way to Iasi we join the queue for security check (no passport control as its an internal flight) then we end up in a little corner of the airport that is quiet and cool. We pause wondering whether we are in the same airport or if we have walked so far that we are in a parallel universe. H goes to buy water but the machine first dispenses Coca Cola and only on her second attempt does she get water (same machine, same button but that's Romania!). Our first Fagaras bar is also purchased.

H sits down and gets out her Gardener's World magazine, looking about as English as you can get without having a large, china, tea pot sitting next to her.

Over the other side of the waiting area (its not a very big waiting area so don't visualise something akin to the Albert Hall, think more small school hall) three men arrive carrying a very impressive trophy that looks a bit like the Webb Ellis Trophy, it has Romanian ribbons on it and is clearly causing something of a fuss. We have no idea what it is about but the fact that they are not been mobbed suggests that it's not football.

What is that phrase about the best laid plans? There now appears to be a problem (and delay) as one person who has booked onto the 5:30pm to Timisoara has not turned up – this means that they appear to have got lost in approximately 400 metres of straight corridor. Whatever the problem is it results in the buses that are shipping us out to the planes being delayed and everything starts to rapidly fall apart. Two of the check in staff start shouting at each other and hands are furiously waved. We sit back and watch the world go by.

It is unclear whether the missing person turns up but Timisoara's loss is Iasi's gain as we all board the happy bus and head over to the aircraft. Disappointingly it's not a propeller driven one as we expected but a rather dull 737-300 with a very excitable Romanian crew (is this their last run of the day?). Safety briefing quickly dispensed with, it doesn't cover life jackets as we aren't flying over the Black Sea and we are off. Lots of rattling and you can almost sense the pilot shouting at the joystick "pull up, pull up" as we climb.

Then it's out with the food trolley that is run down the aisle, at speed, dispensing sandwiches, closely followed by drinks (not hot ones as it would obviously take too long for them to cool down). 20 minutes later and we start our descent, back to Douglas' "Gently lobbed frisbee"[15] – this short flight of under an hour avoids a seven hour train journey, only the price would have swayed us.

We land and appear to be in someone's back garden, such is the size of Iasi *International Airport*, although we are informed that it is the fourth busiest airport in Romania and the most important in the region of Moldavia. It's a leisurely stroll across the tarmac to a baggage collection area that is small enough to fit in my garage (and still have place for a car). As you would expect people are jostling for the best positions close to the carousel (which does look a little homemade). H goes and takes up a position near the wall whilst I grab the body bags, we then form a small *wagon fort*[16] before going outside onto the concourse to try and get into town.

Outside we find the best organised taxi rank in Romania (fact). The taxis have to approach from one direction and are then ferried through in between two large kerbs (or small walls). The impact of this is that passengers must go to the front vehicle and the taxi driver must take them

---

[15] Another Cabin Pressure reference, referring to a short flight.
[16] Apparently, this is what they call the circles made by wagon trains, ours was less impressive but extremely effective at giving us the space we needed to sort gear.

(rather than just sighing). Whilst there must be a way to circumvent this system (and I'm sure someone will) it is not obvious and I'm sure it stops much of the traditional *stealing* of fares.

Sticking to the taxi rank 'rules' we approach the first taxi who, as we expected, has no idea where the hotel we are after is. He talks to his friend in the taxi behind, who does know, and they do a quick passenger shuffle. We hope that this sort of cooperation will be the shape of things to come for the rest of the trip. We leave the airport, which no doubt now has a 'closed' sign now hung on the door, and head off into the hot late afternoon of Iasi. Our somewhat stilted conversation with the driver confirms that it has been hot, dry and sunny over the past few weeks. This is further confirmed by the rather brown looking fields.

Within half a mile of leaving the airport we come across a car crash that is taking up much of the road. Our driver does a quick risk assessment before squeezing his car around it with two wheels in the ditch by the side of the road whilst sounding his horn[17]. We are followed by a few other taxi driving off-road enthusiasts, other drivers just wait for the cars to be moved to one side.

It's a short journey into town and we arrive safe and sound at the Lavric Bistro Hotel where they are happy to accept that Newby Cat is a *nom de plume* and we book into what is a very quirky looking hotel slotting amongst a lot of concrete. It gives the impression of one of those properties where the owner refused to sell and everything has to be built around

---

[17] I believe that sounding the horn must aid traction.

them, it is certainly one of the older buildings on the road. Our room is at the top up some quite narrow stairs with no real passing places, it is very large and has a spare bed in it which appears to be there "because we had the space" It is a handy place to dump the rucsacs, sadly there is no balcony.

Go down to the bar for a Ciuc[18] and discuss how it's great to be back. After much deliberation and having no idea what there is around the hotel we order a very nice anti-pasta platter and a large salad, that we split between the two of us. Another Ciuc and, about 10pm, we turn in, we have run out of steam.

Tuesday 1st August – thank heavens for air conditioning! By setting it to 16° and the fan on full then the room achieves a reasonable temperature. Having set this up last night we sleep very well until the traditional Romanian Dawn Chorus (barking dogs) wakes us at around 3am, then again at 5am. Fortunately, we fall back to sleep during the lull.

8am (6am UK time) we are awake and manage to drag ourselves down for breakfast at 8.30. When we arrived last night we were vague about what time we wanted breakfast and they seemed reasonably happy with that. The hotel appears to mainly have business type people staying here who have already eaten and left for the day and we have our choice of tables. Go for one by the window.

Today is our 30th wedding anniversary and whilst she was reminded on Friday (at a wedding) and she mentioned it again on Sunday (at a wedding) H forgot and didn't get me a

---

[18] Romania beer that is from the Ciuc County

card. This has become something of a tradition so I am not surprised. As always I have remembered, complete with present, so I can sit at breakfast looking really smug!

The inside dining area is a very traditional Romanian bar with what maybe the heaviest chairs I have ever come across. At one point I thought that they were actually bolted to the floor because of how difficult it is to move them. Why so heavy? I suppose that it would make them harder to steal or throw across the bar but I'm not sure that giving your clientele a hernia every time they want to move towards the table is an effective customer retention strategy?

We are brought hot milk with our coffee without even asking. They obviously know what English people are after. This is accompanied by orange juice, homemade butter, jam, bread, yogurt, some weird biscuit things and an omelette that reminds H of the ones that we had had in the mountain hut in 2015.

With the next coffee H starts to turn into a coffee nerd (I can see where our eldest son gets it from[19]) and I am informed that you should drink the top bit off of the coffee first (the crème) before adding milk and drinking the rest. I wait for the next pearl of wisdom about what appears to be becoming a coffee ceremony. Before this can happen we start a rather tangential conversation about the attitude of people we know towards coffee; Michael would give this a big double thumbs up, Andy would look down his nose at it as if to say "Get thee behind me Satan!".

---

[19] At the time of writing Tom is a qualified Beer Sommelier and can't help but comment on the different beers he tries. H has started doing the same with coffee.

Outside, on the terrace, many other people are catching up on their nicotine uptake[20] whilst we try and work out what we are going to do no we are here. Head back to the room to get the maps out.

Whilst we were having breakfast the temperature of our room has risen to 25° even with the air conditioning going[21]. Setting off as we mean to go on we attempt to do yoga (we promise ourselves that we will do some form of exercise every day[22]). Our investigation into Romania's showers recommences and, whilst not quite as powerful as the ones at the Ibis in Bucharest[23], they pack quite a punch. No sachets or bolted to the wall soap dispensers either, just proper old-fashioned bottles of shampoo and shower gel.

Still feeling tired from yesterday's travel, but slightly refreshed after the shower pummelling, we decide to head into town using the miniscule map in the guide book. We soon establish exactly where we are (near the Majestic Hotel) before accidently stumbling across the railway station. Accidently in that it is totally in the opposite direction of where we wanted to be heading and rather than being amongst lovely old buildings we are in a, very, Communist constructed concrete jungle all radiating out from the parking area in front of the station. The station building[24] itself is very grand and we wonder who had the

---

[20] Smoking was banned inside from 2016 but most bars, restaurants etc have small semi-covered areas.

[21] We always take a small digital thermometer with us and the temperatures quoted are based on that.

[22] Spoiler alert…. we don't manage it!

[23] The showers at the Ibis are so powerful they could strip paint.

idea of putting a large drive through McDonalds on one edge!

We turn around and head back towards the town (we will be visiting the station in a few days so can have a tour of it then) and after a short climb we find ourselves at the top of the very large pedestrianised area. From here all of the main architecturally interesting buildings can be viewed, and we make our way to the Metropolitan Cathedral which is both spectacular and huge in equal proportions. Inside doesn't disappoint either where we are struck by the number of pilgrims queueing to be blessed by the remains of Saint Parascheva (apparently on Saints Day, in October, it is heaving with pilgrims, but it seems busy enough now). Leaving the 'Blessings Factory' (as we see it) we go next door to visit St George's Chapel which has an amazing mosaic frieze above the door but, sadly, is closed. We do spend some time here as the marble entrance canopy does give excellent shelter from the sun and its cool.

Next up along the Boulevard of Churches (as we have dubbed it) is the Catholic Cathedral (Our Lady Queen of Iaşi Cathedral) which looks like it was designed in the 1960s/1970s but was built in the 1990s and not consecrated until 2005. Inside there is a lot of stained glass that colours everywhere you look and with its very high roof it certainly is a site to behold. It also has the advantage over the Metropolitan Cathedral in that it is peaceful inside (rather than having lots of pilgrims lining up). The courtyard it is in has limited entrances, by car you have to wait for the barrier to be raised but on foot you walk through a smaller, manned

[24] One of the oldest stations in Romania, built in 1870.

entrance. It is obviously designed to give it a large controlled area in front of the church so it does not become clogged up with cars. At the far end of the courtyard is another church which looks like it is the subject of an archaeological dig. There is a sign on the door that we ignore and just walk in. Inside there are about a dozen cardboard boxes, approximately 4 x 2 x 7 feet long, with holes in the side (similar to those that people bring pets home in, only bigger). We quickly conclude that they contain skeletal remains that are being removed from the site. This is confirmed when we spot one of the boxes that is open. Incomplete skeletons, odd bones etc are in buckets or laid out presumably waiting for the rest to be extricated, some complete ones still lay in the trenches. We take no photos and leave, on our way out we pause to translate the sign we ignored, it says "This Church is CLOSED" (the capitals are theirs), it appears that we have been left alone because we are English and obviously interested in the dig. Maybe locals would have been chased out?

Time for a sit down and a drink. After the usual spying at what people are drinking we end up at the Chocolate Café for some homemade lemonade, H has mint and I have a rather fiery but nice ginger. More importantly it gives us a chance to cool off. On the pavement next to us a pigeon has the same idea, it has found some shade and is refusing to move regardless of the people walking past (who, in their defence, are stepping over it very carefully). Our first 'proper' beggar approaches, then leaves when we ignore him. A visit to the toilet in the 'café' reveals that it is really a large art gallery selling religious paintings that also sells drinks. A large family party go inside and take up all the seating in there, presumably to benefit from the air conditioning.

The pigeon moves its position so it can stay in the shade.

Next stop is Trei Ierarhi Monastery with its very ornate lace like stone work on the outside. Sadly this too is closed, although we doubt that the inside can be more impressive than the outside. We come to the conclusion that Tuesday is the day that all Iasi's religious building close and set off towards the Palatul Culturii (Palace of Culture) where there is a very heavily publicised Torture Exhibition.

The building looks quite close, just beyond the end of the pedestrianised area. We soon discover that it is actually quite a long way but the perspective is changed as it is a huge building!

On the way we pass what is thought to be the oldest building in Iasi (Saint Nicholas Princely Church) although our, brief, research suggests that it has been dismantled and reassembled so we are not sure if that counts. Of course (because its Tuesday?) it is closed, although there are several artefacts of it outside, including the former altar cross. Next to it is a reminder of the 1989 Revolution that looks as if it has had various alterations (plaques) done to it over the years. Was it really only 28 years ago when everything in Romania changed?

Outside the Palace a Japanese lady is trying to take a photograph of the statue. Being the ever-helpful person she is, H walks up and asks if she wants a picture with her in it? Photo taken and H is happy that she has done her good deed for the day.

The Palace suffers from a few problems that many European buildings have in that (in no particular order); bits of it are under construction/refurbishment, a couple of wings are closed due to asbestos and it is really difficult to work out where you pay and which sections you can go in. To make everyone's life easier and give us the right to roam about the building we purchase an access all areas pass for 20RON each then set about wrestling with the audio guide machine which, for 10RON will give us a pair of headphones and a phone number we can access to get the guide. Those of you who read about our original trip will be wondering if Iasi is any different to the, more commercialised, West of the country. Sorry to disappoint but it's the same in the east of the country, the number fails to connect with either of our iPhones or the Romanian emergency phone that we bought last year! Make a mental note to email the museum[25].

So we set out, on our journey without maps, to tour a museum without a guide. Maybe everything will be in English? Maybe not!

We climb up some very impressive marble stairs that are a work of art in themselves and first visit the Art Gallery. Having visited a few different galleries over the years, and several in Romania, we expected to find lots of Communist inspired 'people battling against imperialist servitude' type paintings[26]. We have a pleasant surprise and find that we actually like many of them, at one point we even comment that we would probably allow some of them in our house! As we are on a roll of enjoyment we set about exploring the

---

[25] Never got around to it but still have the packaging.
[26] Type 'Communist inspired art' into a search engine and you'll find what I mean.

rest of the building as our pass appears to let us in everywhere. Highlights include a very nice vaulted room that appeared to be set out for a wedding and a display that was based around technology with all sorts of bits of electronic gadgetry laid out, including the casing for an old IBM hard drive (no internals) and various record players that documented the history of recorded sound. What we failed to find was the Torture Museum, despite extensive investigation (but of course no signs). We even tried looking in the basement but no sign. Oddly what we did locate were a set of car seats that looked as if they had been removed from a Ford Galaxy and then placed in the museum as if they were some form of modern art. As they were tucked away in a stairwell, in a basement and unless *Hidden Art* is the next big thing then I think that its unlikely that they formed part of an installation.

Disappointed at the lack of a Torture Museum, but impressed with the rest of the set up we go outside where it is still ridiculously hot so we head to the Palas Mall, a shopping centre that is tucked around the back of the Palace of Culture. The Mall has exactly what we are looking for, air conditioning! So we have a pause and a wander around looking for water and a camping gas cartridge[27]. Fortunately there is an Auchan Supermarket that has an amazing choice of different types of water, sadly no gas. As there is a lack of benches (unless you are buying from one of the concessions) in the Mall we wander outside to try and find some shade.

---

[27] As we are unable to take gas on the plane we have brought a stove (& pan) but no fuel. In 2016 we relied on Camping Gaz but struggled to get any (eventually found some in Decatholon), this year we have gone with a stove that takes the more available (?) screw type cartridge.

The Mall is wrapped around the back of the Palace of Culture with, in the gap between them, a large formal garden. It is quite odd thing to see this large, modern, shopping centre next to the Gothic spires[28]. As we look back towards the Palace, to the left, there is a modern hotel with a water park much of which is outside so we can see the people swimming but not join them. We find a bit of shade to cool off.

Time to head back to the hotel, but which way? We know that we have come around in a long arc so there must be a shorter way but we want to make sure that we don't drop too far down towards the river and train line (as we will then have to climb back up). Crank up Google maps for an suggested direction (says 20 minutes) and head off making a note to email Google with a suggested improvement of a "shady side of the street" option on the car/train/walk section before doing a bit of pavement hoping[29]. Our route back takes us through some rather run down areas (again Google, maybe an option to avoid them?) and I get scowled at by an old local for taking a picture of a cat in an overgrown garden. The, ever supportive, H scuttles off ahead of me pretending that I am not with her.

We get back to the hotel just in time for my phone battery to run out. It has got very hot and we decide that a couple of hours rest will do us some good. Air conditioning cranked up to turbo power and we wet, and apply, a couple of towels to try and cool ourselves down. At about 7.30 the

---

[28] There is a photograph on Wikipedia of the Palace of Culture with the building site (of what became the Palas Mall) behind it. It does look very odd.

[29] This mainly involves trying to find sections of the pavement that are finished.

temperature is still 30°+ outside so decide to, once more, eat in the hotel. Whilst we get changed we find an English language channel (or at least an English language film) starring Richard Gere, about a book about Howard Hughes[30]. It becomes our background sound for the next hour as we shower and change. We also get some clothes washed and a washing line strung up as we will be here another day[31].

Once more we sit outside at the restaurant where they have lots of fans circulating the hot air. We move to be closer to them but in doing so end up near the large TV screen showing Paprika TV with an Italian (?) equivalent of Jamie Oliver (you'll have to do your own research as to what he was called, we never found out). He appears to be trying to make mini-hamburgers and a chocolate dessert of such a vivid colour that it has thrown the colour balance setting on the TV. You really get the impression that consumption of the dessert would result in such a massive chemical/sugar rush that it could be days before you slept again. We couldn't understand a word of it (Romanian subtitles and in Italian?) but the presenter appears to be enjoying himself. As he disappears off into the credits there is, after the usual batch of adverts, another cooking programme this time with Faye Ripley which us merely dubbed into Romanian.

H's steak arrives together with my mixed grill, accompanied by another huge Greek salad. We toast the last 30 years of marriage with Ursus and, after a long day, treat ourselves to some of the nicest cheesecake I have ever had (it certainly has the thinnest base I've come across). By the time we

---

[30] The Hoax (2006).
[31] When staying longer than one day we try and catch up on the washing (assuming that we can get it dried before moving on).

leave the restaurant everyone else has gone home and we get the impression that the staff have all got their coats on, dimmed the lights and are ready to leave.

A search of the TV channels back at the room reveals very little of interest (not even an odd cooking programme[32]) and we turn in.

Wednesday 2nd August – at 3.18am[33] the dog chorus tunes up ready for the full performance at 4am. H gets up and locates the source of this cacophony as the garden next door where there appears to be some sort of doggie conference going on which involves a discussion with the dogs on the other side of the fence. We try and work out a way to muffle the sound for tomorrow. For the time being we affix iPods and drift off to the World Service Podcasts. The curtains (for once) do their task of keeping the light out and we wake up, properly, at 8am.

Breakfast and once more we opt for the omelette. This then leads to a discussion about how quickly they manage to rustle them up, do they have some pre-beaten eggs or are they all freshly done? Conversation then moves to the Saturday Kitchen Omelette Challenge[34] and how well the chef here would do on it. The omelette is accompanied by coffee and various other things, including an odd looking Italian cake/biscuit called Brio Kakao – this passes the odd

---

[32] Cooking programmes from around the world appear to be playing on Romanian TV 24 hours a day which are mainly dubbed but still look fun.
[33] I checked my phone, hence the accuracy.
[34] For many years on the Saturday Kitchen (a cooking programme on BBC One) the celebrity chefs had to try and cook a three egg omelette in the fastest time, some did better than others!

flavour test although I'm not sure if I'd go out of my way to find them back in the UK. More coffee and H uses a lot of bandwidth updating Facebook with what's been happening.

Our host is lovely and as time goes on his confidence in English improves (as it does with all of the staff). Our Romanian is back to square one after a year away but we, or at least H, are trying to start using it again. The staff seem to get a lot of pleasure out of getting us to pronounce things correctly (repeating it several times) and appreciate our effort to learn the language.

It's going to be another hot day and so, back at the room, we work out how much water we can carry then go down at 10.30 to try and arrange a taxi with the owner (or is he the manager?). We talk to him about Iasi and how we came to be here which he finds fascinating then launches into how wonderful the area is and the many things to see. His enthusiasm is similar to that of Diana Mardarovici who we met on our first day out of Bucharest last year. We comment on how positive everyone is about the place and H compliments him on his command of English. It is so good that we are surprised that he hasn't been to the UK to perfect it (there are very few English visitors and so we have to conclude that he has honed it by watching television).

Taxi arrives and we head off to the Botanical Gardens (Gradina Botanica) which is on a hill to the north of the city. Sadly the taxi lacks any sort of air conditioning and winding the windows down seems to make little difference. The driver has a large towel that he keeps mopping himself with and I wonder how often he has to change it? We have no such luxury and just try and stay still and pant! The journey is not quick enough for our liking, due to the heat, so we are relieved when we arrive outside a very impressive gated entrance and get out into the slightly cooler air, there is almost a breeze. The road outside the gate could do with a little bit of work as we try and avoid the pot holes (actually just holes). Cost of taxi = 20RON.

Through the gates we are treated to the shade of trees whilst we pay at a very nice little pay hut, 5 RON each. We look down the long track towards the centre of the Gardens and realise that shade is going to be limited. Our tour commences and we are pleasantly surprised to see that many of the signs are in English and whilst they are of the "Google Translate" versions of English phrases it does help us considerably.

Did I mention that it was really hot?

First up is an impressive pond with a seating area around it. Not sure what the purpose of the seating area is, especially on a day like this where the wooden slats are hot to the touch and to sit on them may inflict permanent scaring. The pond itself is full of very small frogs and some very well fed carp, not sure if the two are linked. Sadly this area is in full sun so we take pictures and then scuttle back into the shade where we are joined by several brightly coloured European Bee Eaters[35] - looking around we realise that there are lots of them gorging themselves in the sunshine and we seem to have the only ones who are resting. From our shade we now venture out into the formal gardens which appear to be a

---

[35] Merops apiaster – H recognised them straight away. I pointed and said 'bird'.

work in progress with a very heavy presence of David Austin Roses. Whilst we would have loved to have a made a note of some of the specimens the heat forces us back into the shade on the other side as we head into a heavily wooded area with a choice of routes; *Route A* goes, steeply, downhill to a, we think, pond or river area. *Route B*, by contrast heads uphill towards the glasshouses. Our reasoning takes many forms but mainly goes along these lines; "Route A goes to water, water means mosquitoes, mosquitoes means bites......Route A goes downhill, downhill means that we will have to walk back up the hill in the heat". We opt for Route B and, staying in the trees, we arc around walking along what appears to be a disused road which has been the subject of a considerable amount of subsidence/movement. Suffice it to say that it would only be accessible by a four wheel drive with a lot of ground clearance driven by someone who had trained on the Mam Tor Road in the Peak District[36] - following this path eventually brings us to the glasshouse. We are now getting a little dehydrated but decide to try and go inside. Despite the fact that it is meant to be closed on a Wednesday it looks open so we try and get in but as we are about to enter the glasshouse we are told that it is not open by an assistant who is hosing down the plants, the floors, the walls and (judging by the state she is in) herself. Have a quick look at a large map on the wall which gives an indication of where many of the plants are from before we make our excuses and leave.

Oddly there is no café, or refreshment hut, in the Gardens and so, having confirmed that we would be allowed to re-

---

[36] A road that was built on shale and has, over the years, slowly disintegrated.

enter on our ticket we cross the road into another park (Parcul Expoziției) that has numerous cafés and bars. Many give the impression that they are closed, although I think as its so hot everyone just wants to sit in the shade so they are pretending! The Hunter's Bar is open and we order two half litres of mint lemonade which, whilst not as nice as yesterday's offering, is passable[37]. Free wifi in the bar so we have a quick check on what there is to see in the area and H looks up a few different plants that we have seen. By accident I discover that one of the apps we have downloaded has some handy Romanian phrases on it, sadly no translation that would allow us to order some sliced malt loaf[38]. Pay 20 RON for the two drinks and then, as the local clock strikes, we feel the temperature suddenly rise as if someone has turned the heating up – the Dark Sky weather app says that it has gone from 32° to 35° and comments on the lack of breeze, thanks for that.

Further reading of the Iasi app reveals that the city is set on seven hills (like Rome and Sheffield) although it, somewhat strangely, refers to it as the "Original City of Seven Hills".

The toilets are free, clean and well maintained which is reassuring. We conclude that they are maintained by the various cafés rather than being council run, a sort of co-operative toilet. The gent's urinals are best described as open air due to the lack of roof on the building, whether this is by design or accidental is unclear, but it does mean that ventilation is good. Outside of the toilet area appears to be a fridge graveyard with lots of machines in various states of

---

[37] Home made lemonade is very popular throughout Romania and you never find two the same so its great just trying them out.
[38] Old, long running joke.

dismantling scattered about the yard. Any thoughts of disposing them in an environmental way appears to have been forgotten and it is a rather incongruous sight amongst the pleasantries of the park.

Head back into the Botanical Gardens, via a very busy stall selling water. It's still very hot as we walk past the pay booth and we are just waved in by the assistant who is trying not to move too much as this would generate heat. Behind her the ubiquitous fan is whirring away circulating warm air in the small wooden cell in which she is entombed. Go and view the area behind the greenhouse and then push our noses up against the glass to see what we could have seen, had it been open, the answer is lots of green stuff that is running riot over the windows, as expect H identifies a few of them. After about an hour we decide that enough is enough in this heat and we set off with a view to walking back to the town. Using the simple navigational theory that it is downhill to the main part and if we overshoot then we can just find the river and work back.

We step back out beyond the gate with our first priority being to find a route towards town. Secondly, we have to hope that the route is in shade. The obvious shaded route is to follow the series of parks that appear to flank the main road into Iasi and so we cross back into the Parcul Expoziţiei and almost straight away come across a large, free standing, archway that resembles the Paramount Arch in Hollywood (but a bit smaller), closer inspection reveals no plaque or anything that may give reasons for its presence[39]. We cross

---

[39] It is referred to as the Arcul Triumfal and, we think, it was built in 1906. Beyond that nothing.

a minor road into what we think is a further section of
Parcul Expoziției where is it, slightly, cooler. This seems to
be the case in the trees but a nearby thermometer gives a
reading of 43.1°, this seems a little on the high side – maybe
39°/40° max. What is clear is that it is still uncomfortably
hot. At least if we can find some shade it will be tolerable.

In a clearing we come across a collection of statues of
important people (we assume that they are important as
there are statues of them) and once more we comment on
the Romanian's ability to build these. Sadly it is unclear who
these people are as many of them lack plaques giving us a
clue, although we do dip in and out of the shade to visit each
of them in turn. Yes, there is a fountain in the middle of
them as you would expect, surprisingly it is working!

Here the park appears to become a private estate and we are
forced back onto the pavement/cycle lane next to the main
boulevard. We are still outside the main section of the town
where we come across a road junction that appears to mark
where 'concrete meets traditional' from an architectural
point of view. It's a very odd place, in front of us is mainly
traditional buildings but behind us are concrete edifices. We
have no map, refuse to use our phones to get back to the
hotel and rely on our natural navigational ability (it also
means that we can try and stay in the shade). We continue
to head down and find Station Road which we get to by
descending a very ornate staircase which has been
preserved under the new road. At the foot of the staircase is
another fountain together with buildings such as the CFR
Club[40]. Station Road has very much been bypassed by the

---

[40] Căile Ferate Române is the Romanian state railway and the building

new main road and so has become something of an architectural backwater where buildings have been left alone, to crumble quietly. The only traffic we come across, human or vehicular are those of locals who are using it as something of a rat run or race track. Towards the bottom of the road the buildings change yet again to concrete built high rise flats with shops underneath as you would expect in the station area. We pass many rather seedy looking establishments, a few *gentleman's clubs*[41] and the Las Vegas Club. Ahead of us is the station, the other side of a multi-junction roundabout and large car park. It gives the impression that where there was a gap between buildings they just made the road a little wider.

The station is very impressive and can, almost, be forgiven for having a McDonalds drive-through wedged on the left hand side. It's ornate grandeur offers a wonderful vista over the concrete the surrounds it[42]. To the right is a rather odd looking market area that, no doubt, we'll look at getting some food from in the morning. Seeing the station is one thing but getting to it is quite another as we try to work out the logical order for crossing the series of roads in front of us. We go for the right hand side for no other reason than it appears to offer more shade. Inside is cool, bordering on cold due to the marble interior and we are in no rush to move on. The thermometer outside is registering 47° but whilst it has got hotter later in the day it's still not that hot, high 30s at the most.

---

was obviously dating from their halcyon days.

[41] Never quite sure why they are called that. No Gentleman I know would ever go in one.

[42] Built in 1870 it was inspired by the Doge's Palace in Venice and has over 100 rooms.

Inside we go to buy tickets. This is quite a complex procedure that involves, firstly, me handing over my phone with the travel times on and then H asking "Does anyone speak English" as the cashier melts gently in the heat (not even a fan chugging behind her). No one does but we manage to work around it and get the tickets[43]. Checking them I discover that they only show one change (where my app shows two) with a five minutes change over in Bacau. Now, dear reader, if there is anything that we have learned from a month travelling in Romanian previously it is that trains are (1) unreliable and (2) always late. Its Rail Roulette Time again!

Time to eat. We walk past some establishments that offer various types of food but where we think that hygiene is not high on their agenda and certainly aren't showing Food Standards Agency signs. End up heading back to the top end of the old town and find ourselves in Mamma Mia, an odd restaurant which we thought must be part of a chain (but isn't) – crucially it's got air conditioning. The menu is rather disappointing as it lacks any *real* Romanian dishes – I opt for a Moldavian pork dish followed by a very disappointing, mass produced, pudding. The beer selection is similarly uninspiring with the standard choices of Becks, Stella etc. Fortunately I spot an Ursus Black behind the bar. On the plus side lots of Ella Fitzgerald is playing in the background and the toilets are clean. Pay and head back to the hotel, going via a mini-market for crisps, water and beer (Neumarkt at 5RON per litre). The shop is small but very

---

[43] Unlike some other areas we have visited, in Iasi English is not widely spoken (many have Russian as a second language).

well stocked in a wonderfully random way, no idea how the owner finds anything but they do.

Back at the hotel H slumps on the bed, channel surfs for all of five minutes before falling into a deep sleep fully dressed. Tonight's bland film on Paramount is Two If By Sea starring Sandra Bullock and Denis O'Leary about a petty thief and his girlfriend who steal a painting[44]. With this playing in the background and H gently snoring away I re-sort the money envelopes and have a bit of a sort out of gear for in the morning.

Thursday 3rd August – the dog chorus was later than previous days and didn't kick off until about 4am, oddly I was awake before it started almost waiting for it to happen. Just before the chorus there was a shout out and I wonder whether it is started, every morning, manually?

I then fall back to sleep.

8am and its time for breakfast, which is the usual fair of omelette, once more nice and fluffy. H's mosquito bite has started to look very inflamed despite the antihistamines that she has had. I'm not sure that the heat is doing it any good. I have a new bite on my heel exactly where my sandal strap, or the top of my trainer, will go. We'll have to keep an eye on both of these.

The travel today, on regional trains, promises to be a grim experience so we plan carefully to make sure that we have access to everything in the rucsacs without major

---

[44] Don't bother watching it.

dismantling. Gear is appropriately spread out over the beds, floor and table before being packed. The digital thermometer in the room is steady at 23.7° before we crank up the air conditioning to bring it down to 16°.

A little after 10am we shake hands with the owner (remembering that it should be a firm handshake), pay him (approx. £30 a night including breakfast) and head out for the steady walk down to the station in a much more reasonable temperature than we have got used to.

As we reach the station a young, good looking, girl in a red dress walks passed us and is given a very *complimentary* look by one of the workmen who almost falls into the hole that he is supervising the digging of. It's as if we have entered a Benny Hill sketch.

We walk through the station and out onto the platform, passing the long queues at the ticket offices where people were shouting at the ticket sellers (nothing unusual there!). H dumps her rucsac with me and goes off to purchase some food for the journey leaving me to find the correct platform. This I do using a process of elimination as the departure boards are in vague mode. I look at the map and work out that Suceava is north and Bacau is south. We are heading south so platform 3C it is and the R5605. I take out a piece of paper on which I scribble our travel schedule;

      RE5605   to Pascani
      RE5444   to Bacau
      RE5465   to Piatra Neamt

This gives us a twenty minute change over at Pascani (easily do-able even with delays) and a five minute change over in Bacau (not even to save the planet is this change possible, but its ok as I'm sure that there will be another one following on later).

We head for 3C and are met by a guard who asks where we are going, he promptly points at a train 200+ yards from where we think it should be, ie following on from 3A and 3B. I express my belief that he is wrong but we go and check (just in case) and are surprised to find that it is the train we require, full marks for customer service. It's a double decker train and whilst it has obviously seen a lot of miles it is reasonably clean. Can we go upstairs or is that ticket only? Quick check of our tickets confirms that its ok and we head for the steps. On the stairs, effectively blocking our route, is a youth who appears not to want to move and so ends up being clonked by H's rucsac as she tries to squeeze past. He begrudgingly moves to one side and we find seats on the top deck of a nice, clean, air conditioned section of the train which is not packed to the rafters with people. As we make ourselves comfortable the engine goes off (but the air conditioning stays on so we don't question anything). An argument starts on the floor below that gets very shouty. We have no idea what it is about but it sounds serious and we wonder whether the mechanic is involved. Ten minutes later, as quickly as it started, the commotion stops, it goes quiet and the engine starts again. We set off across a very agricultural landscape.

Immediately H moves across to the other side of the train to get a better view and less sun. The view from the top deck is far better than that we normally get and gives us a view over some very odd looking fields. Odd in that they have large walls around them giving the impression that they were actually reservoirs that have been filled in for some reason. Very few sheep are grazing but lots of goats. There is also evidence of the adopting of large scale farming practices as there are lots of pieces of machinery, in various states of usefulness/decay, all poised ready for the upcoming harvest. After saying that there are still lots of people walking the fields doing something.

The toilet cubicle on the train is slowly flooding as it is not possible to turn off the sink tap and the sink has been blocked! This means that everytime we go around a corner the water sloshes out under the door. At least the toilet is still working although it is an adventure to get to it!

Despite leaving Iasi late we arrive in Pascani on time (near enough). The guard appears and tells us that this is our station and we get off. Now the usual challenge of trying to find our connecting train. A quick consultation of the board tells us that we need platform 3B. But isn't that the train that we have just got off of – why did the guard tell us to get off the train if we are just going to get back on it? After a few minutes of total confusion the answer reveals itself in front of our eyes as we see the train being split and a new engine being brought up to it. It appears that Pascani is something of a crossroads so half of the train is heading back to Iasi and the other half is heading to Suceava (to the north and on the list to visit later on in the trip). For a rural backwater Pascani has quite a nice train station. Lots of mechanics are gathering around the train trying to sort out the hydraulics and get everything reconnected – they are being watched and diligently questioned by a boy of about eight. No one is shouting at him to get out of the way and he is learning about how the train works. How safe he is, well that's another matter!

Whilst the train shuffling is going on we are approached by several guards who are asking if everything is ok and where we are going, We even get a smile from a couple of them, have they been on a customer service course? One of the guards is a very tall, well made up female who is walking around as if she is on a photographic shoot for Romanian Trains and we question whether they are due an inspection today?

Get back on the same, now shorter, train and I gesture to one of the fitters that it is very hot. I get a nod, smile and a laugh back. We now head south towards Baccau lunching on the way on pastry wrapped sausages, apples, tomatoes and sheep's cheese. If we were to stay on this train then it would take us towards the Delta as it follows the river south but that area is for later in the trip (all being well). Many of the buildings that we can see from the train have been given a good coating of paint and had some refurbishment so that they look presentable, this is in contrast to the ones we have seen on the Bucharest Plain where they appear to be left to crumble. About 10 minutes out of Pascani the air conditioning unit (or cold air blower) under our table breathes its last, there is a clunking noise and it just stops. At least we are on the shaded side of the train.

The rest of the journey to Baccau is pretty uneventful. A second visit to the toilet reveals that both of them on board are broken and it is only gravity that is allowing the toilets to empty. Oh yes and the locks don't work either. Since leaving

Iasi we have got through our two litre bottle of water and are now on the Decathlon ones. Two stations out from Pascani and we are already ten minutes behind the schedule, this looks like its curtains for our connection but somehow we manage to make up the time and pull into Baccau at 2:28pm. We decide to jump onto another train that is in the station (and is facing in the right direction so looks promising) but checking the boards it looks as if we have missed our connection – we then realise that it hasn't yet gone and is still at Platform 5 complete with guard waving his little green flag.....but how do we get there?

"Underpass!" shouts H and off we set at a brisk canter (running is not possible with the rucsacs we have). I emerge first and am met with the smiling face of a young lad who is beckoning me onboard. "One more" I say gesturing towards H who is now emerging from the underpass, I push her towards our new friend who hauls her on board. The train then starts to pull away and I get the chance to board a moving train in very much a Wild West style![45]

So, we are on a train. Heading in what we think is the right direction. We suspend our celebrations until the guard confirms that we are on the right train. Hopefully this will be the only close call we have of the trip. We open all of the windows in the compartment to try and get some air into an area that, we get the impression, hasn't had fresh air for several months! The angle of the breeze coming through means that the smell of the person just outside our compartment is kept at bay.

---

[45] I make a note to check if boarding a moving train, in a foreign land, is on anyone's "to do" list.

Much of the journey is spent keeping an eye on our gear as we are half expecting one of the likely lads in the corridor to make a play for it and then jump off the train. We close the door to the corridor which has a two fold effect; firstly it puts a physical barrier up to stop Mr Smelly and the Likely Lads getting in and secondly the cool air coming through our window will, hopefully, stay with us.

It's hot, stupidly hot and we have to wedge into the shaded end of the compartment to avoid the direct sunlight (my shorts, my BLACK shorts, are absorbing the heat very well!). The train now appears to decide to run even slower. I do a few calculations and work out that the average speed for this section should be around 23mph but we are spending a lot of time stationery. This reduction in speed causes a reduction in air flow into the train and we start to cook again. We were both aware of how unpleasant it is but neither of us say anything about it. We consume the water and wet my Olympic scarf in order to try and cool us down.

Finally we arrive in Piatra Neamt at a speed only marginally faster than treacle pouring out of a jar and I am reminded of the old adage of "its better to arrive than not at all". We walk outside the station and check the guide book. Our hotel, the Pensiunea Lido, is described as being between the train and bus stations but directions of "step outside and its in front of you" would be more appropriate. We make better time than the train in covering the 40 yards between the station exit and foyer of the hotel. The outside of the hotel looks much better than the guidebook's description and inside we are met by a receptionist who accepts that I am Newby Cat without question. Maybe he is used to odd

English people with big rucsacs turning up and the odd name just adds to our charm.

Our room is very nice but lacks one key feature, that of air conditioning! Not sure how this happened as I thought that it defaulted in on Bookings.Com after last year's problems in Turda[46]. Shower to wash away the sweat from today's journey and wash some of our clothes (we are here for a couple of days so they will have time to dry). On the TV is a National Geographic programme about plane crashes, I fall asleep shortly after starting to watch it. An hour later and, batteries recharged, its time to head into town to get orientated and, more importantly, find somewhere to eat.

The town is built on the side of a hill and has a cable car running over the top of it which goes up to the ski slopes that brings so much tourism to the area. Our hotel is built at the bottom of the hill so it's a nice leg stretch as we set off to the upper part of the town. Quickly discover a Lidl and Billa close to where we are staying. At the top end of the town, where there are various museums they are constructing a large stage, although it is unclear what kind of concert we can expect. After last year's rock concert in Sibiu nothing would surprise us!

We look at the menus of various establishments and find, once more, that many restaurants merely offer pizza and other "Western" foods rather than anything local. In the end we find ourselves at what could best be described as a "pop up" restaurant that is attached to a local's bar. We have

---

[46] Its in the other book! But, basically, we stayed in a room that was in the middle of a swamp and we had the windows open. Result? Loads of mosquito bites.

cheese pancakes (nicer than they look), chips (disappointing) and shredded (very) salad plus a couple of Staropramen draught beers (they had nothing local on offer). Whilst we eat there are a series of loud whoops and cheers from the direction of the stage construction prompting H to comment "They seem to be having more fun than us!". As if to respond to the cheering a live duo suddenly appear and set up in the bar area (a keyboard/vocalist and saxophonist). They then proceed to play a selection of Romanian songs which many of the locals sing along to (or mime along to). We have no idea and so just sway to the music, actually we don't, we just enjoy the spectacle. In the background we can still hear the cheering of the stage team.

We wander back down the main strip which appears to double as a race track for the local motorcyclists, at one point I wonder whether I should start counting laps. There are several bars and restaurants along this route and we pop into one for a Cuic (sadly bottled) and a lemonade. The menu offers "Sommelier Recommended Wines" and we wonder when there will be a beer slot for Tom to take up[47]. It is a little cooler but still warm so it is a pleasant walk back to the Lido.

We have a grump about the lack of air conditioning but at least the double glazing means that we are not bothered by the noise from the taxi rank that lies in the narrow strip between us and the station. H, almost immediately, falls

---

[47] Our eldest son is a qualified Beer Sommelier and is always happy to recommend what beer you should have with different food. Actually he's just happy to talk about beer.

asleep whilst I start watching the Netherlands vs England game (Women's Euros).

Considering how little exercise we have taken today I'm surprised how tired we are. We have to blame the heat[48].

Friday 4th August – the lack of air conditioning does mean that it is a warm night but not too bad. Once more the double glazing helps us, so the dog's chorus is very muffled.

6am and the first train whistle sounds – somehow this does manage to penetrate the double glazing, it again sounds at 7am and then 8am. Fortunately we manage to fall asleep in between the toots and don't start to move until 10am. It is clear that yesterday's long journey, in an oven, has really taken it out of us. H especially is struggling to get motivated. This morning's awful film is Tower of the First Born starring Ben Cross, Peter Weller and Iona Skye. We look up the reviews and decide it's not worth the bother. Basically they are all horrible people who, mostly, die at the end![49] Time to get moving.

Whilst the hotel does appear to serve breakfast it is extra and our previous experience suggests that we should go out to eat where the choice may be a little better. Once more onto the main boulevard up through town where we reject the first café as it appears to resemble a Far Eastern opium den with lots of men standing outside smoking away (this is directly underneath a non-smoking sign!). Find a book shop and buy a map of the area that we are in. Whilst it's not a

---

[48] Just in case we hadn't mentioned how hot it had been.
[49] Best review said "It took me four attempts before I could watch the whole thing without falling asleep."

walking map it does give us a lot of information about the area. A coffee and a sit down at the Select Restaurant whilst we try and work out what we are doing over the next few days. The guide book comes out and a second coffee is ordered (we even manage to work out the wifi code for the café as well).

Many options are available to us from here, but we need more advice. Do we take the risk and visit the place that offers so much but has a habit of delivering so little? Do we go to the office of dreams in the hope that our dreams will be fulfilled? That's right, we are wondering if we should visit the Tourist Information Office? Its located in the middle of a car park and resembles a small AA sales office. We go in and are met by Mr Enthusiasm who gives us a potted history of the area (actually of most of Romania) and, when we tell him our plans, he even offers us a lift up to near Suceava this evening as he is going to visit his in-laws. Whilst we are touched by the offer we decline as we are hoping to go up towards Bicaz for a camp and a wonder around. Our main question of "can we get gas anywhere?" is met with a blank look but we decide that as we are not going high then we can live on cold food and bought coffee.

We ask him where to eat and he recommends Nenea Iancu saying that the bloke who founded the brewery is a sort of 19th Century Mr Bean (his comparison, not ours). We are totally overwhelmed with the information that we have fired at us over the next 40 minutes and then head off to have a look at another restaurant that he says is overrated. We decide that its not for us and carry on to try and look for the brewery (which is closed when we get there).

Out of the corner of her eye H spots a fishing shop – surely they will sell gas for camping stoves? No, they don't, but point us in the direction of the shopping mall which is next door. No joy in the shopping mall although it does appear to sell everything from mobile phone covers to wigs (lots of wigs!) and the obligatory supermarket in the basement! We do use the toilets in the mall but don't buy anything (for the record the toilets were very clean).

Head to the top end of town where all of the museums are located. At the top of some steps, just beyond where we had had dinner yesterday we stop at a bench in the shade for a few minutes. We are approached by a lad who is running the nearby pop-up bar.

"Do you want a drink?"
"No, thank you".
"OK, you are English?"
"Yes"
"Is this your first trip here?"
"To Romania? No, its our fourth"

There is a pause, a big pause. Paws so big that a large polar bear would have been happy with them. We look at each other knowing the question that is about to be asked but we wait for it anyway knowing that it will amuse us.

"Why are you in Romania?" Yes, it's the question we were expecting and we are amused, almost punching the air!

We explain why we are here and he, sort of, accepts it (actually he looks at us as if we are totally crazy). H asks after our new friend and what he is doing here. It turns out that he has written a stage play and is trying to get produced at the local theatre. He recommends that we try and go to the Youth Theatre while we are here and points out where it is. We ask after the stage and concert that is about to take place but he shows total contempt for it saying that his generation "don't really like that" although he doesn't make it clear who his generation is, or what specifically they don't like. We mention the festival in Cluj that is taking place this weekend but he just glazes over and wanders back to the bar area to polish some more glasses!

We continue our, much interrupted, walk up to the art gallery where we are met by a very pleasant assistant who explains that we have to purchase tickets somewhere else before coming back to do the tour. Excellent spread of work by Romanian artists (some of whom were very avant garde) and a few who lived through both the Communist and post revolution periods, although their style does not seem to change.

Tickets for the clock tower work on a similar system except we are followed out to the tower and let in with the instruction "can you tell us when you have finished so we can lock up again". It has an interesting history although we struggle to work out, geographically, where everything is when we look at the old maps. It is only later that we discover that the tower is much older than many of the other buildings in the square and certainly older than the church.

Both the church (which is very Orthodox) and the tower are much more impressive from the outside and we are reminded of our teenager friend from earlier who said that young people don't want to go into a church "...where you have to go around and lick each wall!...". Ignoring this warning we go in to find a very small, unimpressive area which is dominated by two large signs saying "No Photos" and a woman who is mopping the floor as if she is cleaning the deck of a warship. Leave and head for the Cucuteni Neolithic Museum where there are lots of archaeological finds from a nearby dig. Even though there is very little information in English it is absolutely fascinating with us filling the gaps with quick internet checks. As we are about to leave the top floor exhibition we are approached by a lady in her early 40s who says "Can I be of any help?" - it turns out that she was involved in many of the digs (we later find out, via a photograph of her, that she is a local university professor who was the lead on some of them) and talking to her really brings the exhibits to life. Her English is excellent and she outlines that there is a real lack of knowledge about the Neolithic Period of history and the problems they have trying to identify what different items are. She also suggests that if we have enjoyed this museum then we should head down to the Metropolitan Museum which is just down the road so, following our standard rule, we do just that[50].

Our arrival at the Metropolitan Museum causes chaos as the ticket office is not manned and the only member of staff that we can find does not speak English and has no idea how the ticket system works. He makes a panicky phone call with sweat running down his face (it is hot). A pause follows before telling us (using the medium of hand gestures) that we should look around whilst we wait for the assistant to return (we have no idea where they have gone) and then pay

[50] We have always said on these trips that, where possible, we will be driven by what locals suggest we do and where we should visit.

on exit. We get the impression that he is happy for us to go around for nothing but is just towing the party line. So we set off and are immediately rewarded with an excellent exhibition which has a potted history of the area dating back to 5,000BC. OK, so there is a bit of gap between 1,000BC and 1,200AD but most sections are covered. I make a mental note to read up more fully on the history of the area[51]. Some rooms are closed as its late in the day which is a shame as the rest of the museum is a delight. Yes, we do pay although the, now found, assistant appears to be a little unhappy that we are wanting to hand over money.

As we walk down the steps from the museum we realise that we haven't eaten anything since the snack we had at breakfast. We cast our minds back to the recommendations of our friend at the Tourist Information Office (hut) this morning and head for Nenea Iancu where H has trout and I have smoked sheep pastrami. All washed down with what is advertised as a "local beer" on the menu. It then goes on to say that it is brewed *locally* by *locals* using *local* water, under German tutelage and I find myself wondering if this is some sort of philosophical a question with the word discuss just put at the end.

Soon after we sit down we realise that its Friday night as the bar starts to fill up with office parties and we try and work out what each group does. Our first Friday night in Romania also brings with it our first little girl beggar who comes and whines next to us. I explain, politely, that if I can ignore a puppy with its head on the table then I'm pretty sure that I

---

[51] Like many people of my age our education regarding the history of that area is limited to everything post 1948 and the Cold War.

can ignore her. Eventually she gets bored and moves onto the local office parties from where she is chased off by the staff. We are treated to some classic 80's pop including Rio, Living on a Prayer and Wake Me Up.

As we get towards the end of the meal we hear music from up the road that is getting closer (ie louder). In turns out that we are on the route of a Youth Music Festival which is running this weekend and this is the parade at the start of it. H wanders out onto the route to get some photographs of the people in their national costumes. Most of Europe is represented including a large contingent from Greece.

With the parade over and the office parties getting into their rhythm we pay up and head back to the hotel via the supermarket for some water, fruit and (most importantly, a bag of ice). At the room we spread out the map and start trying to map out the next few days travel (we are now getting to the end of the pre-booked part of the trip, after here we are into unplanned territory).

Sunday	Bicaz and walk up to the cabana/campsite
Monday	Wild camp or stay at a refuge
Tuesday	Back to Bicaz and out to Bacau
Wednesday	To Gura Humorului to visit the painted monasteries

At best the route looks, without our own transport, ropey and we run the risk of being stranded at the top end of Bicaz. It is a high risk strategy that could leave us at the end of a dead end valley with no way out[52]. We turn over the paper and put together a plan B

Sunday	Train to Gura Humorului
Monday	Monasteries
Tuesday	Vatra Dornei – Ilva Mica – Rodna and wild camp at Rodna

Again it gives us a vague plan before we start to head west for, hopefully, some hill time. We have another look at doing a dash into Moldova to the east or Ukraine in the north but conclude that all we will be doing is spending a day heading into the country and a day heading out of the country just to get a picture of us standing at the border and "country bagging" was never part of the ethos of this trip.

Now we have a plan we need to book accomodation[53] - sadly we are let down by both Bookings.com and AirBnB (both booked up) and end up taking a step into the unknown with LastMinute.com with somewhere that is about 1 ½ miles out of town (Gura Humorului). No food is listed and we are booked into a "Junior Suite" – the photo on the site looks good so we try and be positive.

Around midnight we finally snuggle down.

Saturday 5th August[54] – trains are obviously on their weekend schedule as there is no 6 or 7am train sounds. The

---

[52] Any train times we can find are vague and there is a suggestion that the line is subject to regular closes.

[53] We find it much easier to book accommodation before getting train tickets as it motivates us to get there!

[54] In my diary I have already started getting confused over dates as I have written 5th (?) for today's date.

earliest sound we get is the church bells at 8am (and then again at 8.30).

Up, exercise[55] and shower (the shower is positioned down an odd corridor from the sleeping area with a very slippy floor). H complains about a poor night's sleep whilst the bite on my foot has flared up considerably as my sandal strap has been rubbing on it. On the plus side my big toe nail (that I badly bruised last December and has been strapped up for the last few weeks) has fallen off so no more messing about taping it up[56].

With the next few days sorted we now have one day to get out and about in Piatra Neamt to see the sights. After some discussion (ok, very little) I am told that we are going on the gondola that crosses the town up to the top of the hill as, I am told, we will have great views. I counter with at least six good reasons why I don't want to go on but am told, "you'll be safe", "it'll be fun" and H's killer argument of "I want to go on it and I'll look after you". I lose the argument and ten minutes later we find ourselves standing in the queue for tickets! On the plus side I have negotiated a one way only trip with the intention of walking down.

Whilst not exactly heaving it is quite busy and so we are surprised to find that we get a cabin to ourselves, surprised but happy as it means I can gently whimper in the corner. I put my headphones in and listen to my fear of heights tracks (they are called something like "ways not to die on a cable car"[57]. It seems to help and I am informed by H that, 8

---

[55] We do some stretches.

[56] Sadly this resulted in an in-growing toes nail that plagued my running times up until the end of the year.

minutes later, I look a lot better than I normally do after such an ordeal. We dock in a very undignified manner, in that we seem to just crash into the upper station. Like many of these cabins the doors open and we have to get out whilst it is still moving, how people do it with skis I don't know.

I have to admit (but I don't tell H) that it is worth it for the views over the town as we head over the roofs. At the top we are rewarded with spectacular views in all directions, down towards Piatra and then up the valley towards the hills above Bicaz that we were originally heading for, they'll be there on another occasion if/when we return[58]. There is also something in the sky that we haven't seen for some time – we double check and consult the internet.....apparently they are clouds.

The summit station (it's not on the summit but it is a station) is a bizarre place that is obviously more active in the winter months. There are many shops selling the usual tourist tat and a large igloo style "tent", which is sealed off, and we conclude that this is something for the skiers. From this area we realise that there is something odd just below us. There is a large breezeblock construction built into the hillside. What is it? No idea, a partially built hotel perhaps or potential retail outlets? What is obvious is that it is very much the elephant in the room as none of the staff will comment on it! We too ignore it and carry on looking round.

---

[57] Or maybe something more sensible!
[58] Places such as Bicaz become something of a Shangri-La to us as they are only, easily, accessible by car and that seems against what are trying to do. Maybe we'll do a full car tour of the country some day?

H comes across a large group who appear to be in a surreal comedy sketch similar to Father Ted where they are trying to do a group photograph but, in order to do so, they are taking lots of photos! Using sign language she asks if they want a group photo and is presented with about a dozen cameras. She makes a mental note not to be so helpful in future. To add to the confusion there is a professional photographer wandering around taking pictures of everyone and everything, presumably to print and sell (although we never see any on display). We head off in search of some breakfast and coffee.

H is still bitter about the price we paid at the coffee shop in Bucharest Airport and so, everywhere we go, I am subjected to a "I'm willing to pay….for coffee here!". Here, with the view, two lovely omelettes and four coffees we pay under a tenner! It makes her a little happier but doesn't fully heal the wound! The café areas are built on a raised terrace around the edge of the hill to maximise the views. The summer months are when maintenance appears to takes place and we observe a couple of blokes repairing some floorboards using a chainsaw and nailgun whilst wearing sandals and observing very few health and safety rules. Fortunately no accident occurs and, having picked our way past them. we set off to try and find the path down.

Once more we are reminded that Romanian footpaths fall into one of two distinct categories. Firstly the well signposted, well trodden routes that anyone could follow and, secondly, ones that are vague for three quarters of the way but then like motorways for the rest of it (the three quarters are not necessarily all together). Today we find ourselves on the second type as we stumble about trying to find where the path even starts. From the cable car we could see it so we know it exists but where? We stumble across what appears to be evidence of a mountain bike race, from when we don't know but there are some taped sections and a few arrows. We conclude that this is the top of the path down and walk along a very nice downhill section, not too technical but with some very flowing corners. The cycle track goes into the trees just below the "hotel" where we pick up what appears to be the service track up to the cable car station. That this is the way down is confirmed shortly after when we meet the supply truck making heavy work of getting up the slope (and making a lot of dust and fumes in the process). From one of the corners (hairpins?) we see a path that goes off to what looks like a clearing in the trees so we go and investigate and find one of the ski runs that has been cut out of the forest. Sadly it is too steep to follow down so we retrace our route back to the main track and continue down. For much of the descent we are on our own, a couple of teenagers on mountain bikes (one a half decent Specialized) come flying past us, there helmets strapped to their handbars and then disappear into the woods as quickly as they have appeared.

It's a very long descent and our first sign of the outskirts of town is when we come across a large carpark where a family are well and truly encamped in the picnic area with a large feast spread out on the tables. So far we have been well protected from the sun because of the trees but as we reach the zoo, and the real outskirts, we are back into the sun baked streets. Just beyond the zoo we pause by a shop (in the shade) to work out where we are, and more importantly where we want to be! According to Google Maps we are near the mountain shop but the lack of road name signs and only occasional building numbers results in us doing several laps of the same area before I sit H in the shade and head off to do a full trawl of the road. Working logically I careful work out exactly what the building numbers should be (if they had them on display) and, down a small alleyway, come across a building with the sign Romanian Mountaineering Association. The building is well and truly closed!

Head back to the Tourist Information where a different assistant suggests that the campsite may be a good place to get gas but then gestures that they may only sell large gas bottles. Her hand position appears to indicate the sort that you get in a house! We ask after the weather forecast for the next few days and it looks like its going to be rough where we are heading but its currently 40° (she gets more pleasure out of telling us the second piece of information than the first!). We scuttle over to Cafeteria Central for a Sprite and a cool off. H logs onto the wifi and we find out that it's raining back home!

Now we have a plan for the next few days there are a few things to sort out. First is to get some food for the journey, so it's to Lidl to try and get some food that "will last" (ie not melt in the heat!). Then it's to the station to try and get tickets for tomorrow's journey. Confusion reigns as the cashier thinks that we want to travel straight away and has us leaving at 22.46 and getting into Gura Humorului at 6.28 tomorrow morning. When we explain that we don't want to leave until Sunday morning she looks happier (maybe the night trains aren't that good or she is concerned about our safety).

Our original choice of trains gives us a 6 minute change over in Suceava and we ask the obvious question, "Is this possible?" She doesn't even hesitate before shaking her head and waving her hand. We assume that this means no and ask after the next best alternative. This gives us a stopover in Suceava and an arrival time in Gura Humorului of around 5pm. Back to the hotel for some downtime, the temperature has dropped but is still in the mid 30s. Police Academy 2 on the Paramount Channel!

Hoping that it has cooled down (it hasn't) we head out at about 6pm with a view to visiting the campsite on the other side of the river from the town. This involves walking, for some way, along the side of a road which is heavily populated by funeral directors, at least twenty in a long line by the side of the river. The businesses that aren't funeral directors are all related to the funeral service, such as masons with a grand display of headstones outside. The one oddity in this collective is, at the very end, a car spares shop which has a spectacular selection of headlight bulbs.

Cross the bridge over a very silty river, the sort of colour that you wouldn't want to swim in although it does seem to have a strong current as well so I wouldn't fancy my chances. Looking up the river we can see one of several hydroelectric plants which break up the river all the way up to the large dam at the head of the valley. What we can't see is another bridge that will cross the river into the far end of the town but conclude that it must be there.

The houses on the south side of the river fall into two categories; those that have been well maintained over the years, regularly painted etc and then those that the owners have just tried to keep in one piece (sort of). Looking at some of these I think it would be cheaper to just to knock it down and build a new one rather than try and *renovate* (although the word renovate does not appear to exist in the Romanian vocabulary, only patch up when necessary).

From the direction of the campsite a group of teenagers appear who seem to be on some sort of forced march judging by the pace they are going at, and that they are all walking in step (not quite marching but very close). Like us they are having to cross from side to side to try in order to find the pavement (where it exists) or, more likely, avoid the sections where the road just falls into a ditch. Eventually we reach the campsite to find a distinct lack of tents but a lot of parched earth. What there is an abundance of is log cabins, although judging by the number of people sitting outside of them it would appear, on a day like this, that they are merely large wooden ovens[59]. Whilst the swimming pool is almost empty the bar area is not with everyone trying desperately to get in the shade. H comments that she doesn't think it's the sort of site where you would get a good night's sleep. The only shop we find does not appear to sell gas and, having looked at the queue, decide not to wait and ask[60].

At the far end of the campsite are some turnstiles suggesting that in days gone by you had to pay to enter the area. They appear to have been abandoned a long time ago and some of them have been partly dismantled so we guess they didn't work too well. Just beyond the turnstiles is a pedestrian

---

[59] More of this later on the trip when we head to the Black Sea.
[60] It is one of those campsite shops that, at first sight, appears to sell everything but then you realise that it sells very little. In fact it appears to mainly sell beer.

footbridge which is built to the same (over engineered) design as the ones we encountered in the Turda Gorge in 2016 although here there are more planks that are in need of replacement. A large sign at the far end of the bridge suggests that the bridge is sponsored (was sponsored?) by the Ursus Brewery which is quite apt as we did feel a little drunk walking across it!

The railway line that goes up the valley from here was built to carry raw materials to build the hydroelectric plants and, since then, only appear to have occasional use so we feel like archaeologists when we come across the tracks. They are still greased (just) and local enquiries suggest that trains do still run along them but no one will commit to a time that they do, whether they carry passengers or how far up the valley they go[61]. Across the tracks we discover why the centre of town is quiet during the day, it's because there is a large shopping centre complete with a Carrefour and a cinema. Of course, most importantly, it is air conditioned so in we go.

In the Carrefour we, at last, find gas! Sadly it's the Camping Gaz *punctureable* type which is useless for the stove we have[62]. We briefly consider buying a new stove but scrap that idea on the grounds of weight and decide that what we need is a real camping shop. Sadly they are quite thin on the ground

---

[61] It is unclear whether this is because they don't know or don't want to give out information that may show the country in a bad light (something we are becoming more conscious of)

[62] Roughly speaking there are three different types of camping gas cartridges; the Camping Gaz Punctureable ones, the Camping Gaz valve type (which we had in 2016) and the MSR valve type (which we have in 2017). None are freely available.

in this part of Romania, there are several Decathlon stores and that is about it. After the disappointment of the Carrefour we head to the food court which is similar to those in just about any out of town shopping mall with various *Western* or *Westernised* foods on offer (including KFC). This just doesn't seem right in such a culinary rich country so we abandon the air conditioning and head back towards town remembering to just keep the river on our right. This brings us out at the large car park near the Tourist Information where we head to the Connection Bar. They don't appear to be doing food, so it's just a quick Ursus before we decide on Dina Doner, a reasonably clean looking kebab place on the main strip. A sultry waitress approaches our table, hands us the menu and then goes through it, pointing at most items on the main page saying "No!" or "Not that!" After this very theatrical display she realises the lack of choice and gestures to the whole page and says "No!"

Having taken careful note of everything that is off H gestures to the menu saying, hesitantly, "This one?" and Little Miss Happy disappears into the kitchen area. We are then treated to a very vocal discussion between the waitress and the chef? Is this the point that we leave or do we stand our ground? Decide to wait and she returns with a smile on her face say "Da!" a lot. We order two and she puts up her hands as if to surrender. It takes us a few seconds to realise that she is holding up her fingers to indicate that it will take ten minutes. Happily we order 7UP (diet options not available) and log onto the wifi. My phone battery dies but I can't be bothered to head back to the room for the battery park and sit back to listen to the continued shouting in the kitchen. Behind the counter a large TV appears to be showing adverts on a loop.

I think that the last thing that the waitress (and the mad chef in the back) wants at this point in the evening is a large party arriving and so that's exactly what happens. We sit and wait as the noise coming from the kitchen gets louder, expecting at any moment the waitress to storm out or, at least, hit one of the group who have just arrived.

The surrealness is cranked up to eleven as Wagner's Ride of the Valkyries suddenly plays over the loud speakers that had previously been advertising soap! The TV screen is blank and we brace ourselves expecting something to happen. Nothing does, and by nothing `I mean the food doesn't arrive either. Forty minutes after the initial ten minute quote is given the food arrives and before you ask, no, it wasn't worth waiting for. We are served some barely cooked chicken which comes with some cooked barley which H says tastes as if it was flavoured with a very salty stock cube. Not a meal to remember Peatr Neamt for!

Back at the room the Police Academy non-stop filmathon (is that even a word?) continues whilst we plan tomorrow's journey north.

In the UK Usain Bolt finishes third in his final individual event.

Sunday 6th August – at about 4am Casey Jones was sounding his whistle like it was some sort of plea for help but then stops after about 10 minutes. Around 6am a small dog chorus starts up (but doesn't last very long).

My phone informs me that today is Hiroshima Day and the anniversary of the first HTML website being posted.

7.30 and we finish packing ready to move out. Almost a week in and we are getting better at packing for travel. Out of the hotel we head out into the cooler morning air than we are used to and walk across the road to the station.

Get a coffee from a very nice station café (why hadn't we discover this place before?) before setting out to try and find our seats (81 & 82) on board one of the two carriages that are waiting for us. After getting all of our gear stowed we are informed by the guard that we are on coach 6 not 7 as we thought. Gear taken down from racks and off we go in search of the other seats 81 and 82.

We quickly locate seat 82, it is next to 84 and 86. Opposite seats 83 and 85. It appears that 81 is the corridor! H strikes up a conversation with a couple of blokes who are just heading for Bacau, it would appear they have just had a night out in Peatra Neamt. The train is, relatively, full but it is at least (1) cooler and (2) better maintained than the one we travelled in on a few days ago. We assume that the train is so busy as it's the first day of the holiday as many work on Saturday.

We arrive in Bacau and, after the respectable architecture of Peatra Neamt, find it something of a shock to be back in the world of Communist Concrete. The station, one of the busiest in the country, is very utilitarian. H looks at the platform that previously she had run across and almost has flashbacks to being manhandled onto a moving train. We have about an hour to kill before our train leaves and so head outside and find a nice café next to the station where we have the usual strange looks, apparently they have very few people of our age with big rucsacs passing through! Looking around it appears that this is the café where people come to try and get rid of their hangovers after a Saturday night session.

We finish our coffees and head back into the station for 11am. Check the board to find that our train is not listed (on departures or arrivals) but there are people waiting for it on the platform that had previously been listed. Is the train late(likely)? or has it gone through early(unlikely)? We check where it has come from and when we discover that its come from Bucharest (about five hours away) we conclude that it is likely to be late.

Much to our surprise it arrives at 11.20, only 5 minutes late, and we scramble on board – there are only four carriages but we are on carriage number 463, which takes some locating. The Guard points us in the direction of the rear of the train and, we head towards a wall of noise. We have come across every teacher's holiday nightmare, a hundred plus kids going on summer camp! No wonder the guard was happy to point us in that direction as he was staying down at the quiet end. The noise level from these 8-10 year olds is phenomenal and echoes around the carriage. Step forward H who just glares at a few of them who are infringing on our space and they scuttle back to their seats[63]. Our seats are, of course, occupied by someone else but they move and our rucsacs are safely stored under the seats. We settle in with H reading her book on gins and, rather unsubtly, snuggling into the air conditioning unit.

As we head north the cloud is sweeping in and it appears to be getting cooler (or at least cooler than we are used to!), is the weather starting to turn? Whilst the kids are a distance away they are still very noisy so its iPods on and books out as conversation is not possible. In the middle of all of this the man next to us manages to fall into a deep sleep.

Two stops out from Suceava the teachers (?) start to round up their charges and get them ready to disembark. A task made more difficult as there are three stations in Suceava (North, West and Central) and whilst they hesitate, we scuttle off and get some shade underneath a beautiful

---

[63] This is a gift that many primary teachers appear to possess. I'm sure that there's a PhD study in there somewhere.

canopy on the platform. Sitting on our rucsacs we have the opportunity to watch the kids disembark and be formed up into little groups before being lead off to who knows where. Once on the platform they suddenly become calm, maybe they have had the "don't mess around on the station or you will die!" speech?

With a couple of hours to kill we decide to head off to a nearby shopping centre that we have located on Google Maps. We know roughly where it is but there is no obvious way over the railway line so, rather than risking it, we follow a very circuitous, Google suggested, route. This takes us through some rather rough looking areas where we stand out more than normal as it's a Sunday afternoon and the closest the locals appear to be getting to exercise is just sitting outside drinking beer, certainly not wandering around with a big rucsac. One of the roads we follow is so quiet that, in the middle of it, there is a dog that is fast asleep. After about fifteen minutes we find ourselves crossing a bridge over the railway lines and notice that we could have just walked down the, very long, platform to get there. From the bridge we have a great view up and down the tracks as well as one towards the shopping centre, which includes a Decatholon (maybe gas?). As we head towards it we see a Dedemans store with a large posting outside showing all sorts of stuff that they sell. Whilst its mainly building equipment (and I'm not in the market for a cement mixer.... although for the price I did try and work out how I could get it home) it does also sell camping gear – gas?

Leaving H sitting on a bench outside with the rucsacs I set off into the barn of a building and, more by luck than judgement, stumble across the camping section. It's so small that I wonder if it's the end of the season! There is gas and it looks like the right sort. The only problem is that it has a seal on the top so I cannot inspect the threads. Fortunately an assistant arrives and, mainly, using hand gestures I put over what I am after. He calls for assistance from a colleague and the three of us continue with the rather odd ritual of trying to work out if this is the correct gas – this almost involves one of them piercing a gas cartridge with a key to demonstrate how that sort works. Decide to buy the resealable one, if its wrong its wrong!

Outside I approach H like a victorious athlete, proudly holding the cartridge above my head. The next task is to remove the seal, I have chosen wisely and we are safe. Shoulder our rucsacs again and head off to Decatholon, walking past a man who has been fast asleep on the bench during our entire visit to Dedemans. Rain threatens as we near the shopping centre which is almost identical to the one in Peatra Neamt and we wonder if this is a standard format that they use in Romania[64]. In Decathlon we are asked to leave our rucsacs with the security guard, although not sure why as it would be very difficult to wedge stolen goods into them as they are packed to near capacity. A wander around reveals no dried food and only the blue butane gas cartridges. In fact it's quite poorly stocked from what we have become used to.

Collect our luggage and head outside where there is evidence that it has been raining whilst we have been in the store, fortunately it's not now so our jackets can remain stowed away[65]. Our route back to the station is much

---

[64] It is.

shorter as we have discovered that there is a way into the lower end of the platform[66].

I risk a coffee from the machine to use up some of the change that we have amassed over the few days that we have been here (1.5RON) and find it oddly drinkable (despite the excess of sugar and lack of milk!). H, more sensibly, goes with water, which tastes like water.

On the platform there is what appeared to be a shrine to a police officer (?) with lots of candles and a photograph. Whilst there is no text stating what it is for the way people are pausing at it suggests that it is a recent addition to the platform furniture. Eventually our, regional, train arrives and we are back to basics on the seating front. Another friendly guard confirms that this is the right train and we clamber on board as the rain starts to fall. It is still hot!

According to the timetable it's only an hour from Suceava to Gura H but, due to the state of the train, it seems a lot longer and we are happy to get off at our stop (according to our tickets) – we are promptly met by a guard who ushers us back onto the train saying "wrong station!", in fact 'ushers' could be replaced by 'sccoped' due to the nature of his gestures. It turns out that we want Orsa Gura Station, which is a little further round, and six minutes later we are in the right place. It's now raining heavily and, having no idea where our accommodation is, we jump in the first taxi. Our driver says "No problem, 10RON", we insist on him using the

---

[65] Getting the jackets out isn't a problem but travelling with wet gear is.
[66] As with most platforms in Romania it is ridiculously long and could accommodate a train probably 400+ metres long. Apparently to accommodate the entire population suddenly arriving!

meter and set off firstly out of town and then down a long dirt track under the impression that we have been kidnapped due to the lack of buildings in the direction we are going. Five minutes later and we screech to a halt in a large cloud of dust outside what we thought was a pension. In fact it is a rather swish looking hotel and our room, which is grandly labelled a Junior Suite has a separate lounge area (which can double as a bedroom), 2 televisions, 2 balconies and a state of the art shower cubicle that blasts hot water at you from all directions – all this for around £50 a night, room only (many thanks to LateRooms.com). It's been a long day so, after a little thought we decide to head for the restaurant (which is surprisingly empty) for what is the best meal of the trip so far. This is reflected in the price but still great value. We even sample some of the local wine.

Then it's back to the room to sort/wash gear and watch Red 2 on one of our televisions!

Week Two

Monday 7th August – We've been travelling for a week now and are well and truly embedded in Romania. Last night there was an electrical storm and the welcome rain brings the temperature down to a more reasonable level.

We breakfast on the front balcony overlooking the car park and watch lots of people leaving and heading off to who knows where. H points out that the view from the other balcony is better (although currently being hit by rain) and we agree to move the chairs later. Our plan for today is to visit the two Painted Monasteries in the area. Firstly, we are going to make our way up to the Manastirea Humor. Then make our way to Manastirea Voronet, from where we should be able to walk back to the hotel. This plan is dependent on numerous factors, not least that the Rough Guide's vague instructions about where we can catch a Maxi Cab up to Voronet are correct.

Taxi booked with the hotel and, despite, the distance we are from the main part of town, it arrives very quickly (maybe Gura isn't quite the hot bed of a visitor's centre we thought it was[67]) and we get in. As we struggle to locate the seat belt sockets under the rear seat covers the driver turns to us and says not to bother as, "Its Romania!", he adds to his confidence by spending most the journey looking and talking at us even though we are in the back. Our conversation with our new found, taxi driving, friend takes a strange turn when he thinks that we are French! Not sure where this

---

[67] To say that we were unable to book any accommodation in town it doesn't seem that busy.

assumption comes from. After much discussion/confusion we agree to be dropped off where the driver feels is where we want to be (this is helpful as we have little/no idea where we need to be for the Maxi-Cab). In order to get there he has to execute a u-turn on the main road, which he does without hesitation, or noticing the cars coming towards us.

But first coffee!

Find a pleasant pop-up café on the main strip and we are brought another sludgy cup served up with some milk which appears to be on its way to becoming cheese but its officially, drinkable....just! Look for the Rough Guide but realise that, together with my waterproof, we have left it in the room. So it's onto the free Wifi, and trawling H's memory, to find out how we get to the monasteries. We soon establish that transport leaves from outside the Best Western hotel in the centre of town every hour or so. The hotel is a huge, barely full building near a large roundabout that slows all traffic through Gura down – why the Best Western was showing as full when we tried to book I don't know.

It starts to rain which is a problem as my jacket is back at the hotel and so I buy an umbrella from a corner shop (of which there are many). Outside the Best Western there is an area where taxis (of all sizes) are gathering so we go and inspect who is going where. Not wanting to make choosing a taxi easy none of them have a notice (normally a piece of card) in the window that may give a clue to their destination, so H uses all of her communication skills and gets in the first MaxiTaxi, "Does anyone here speak English?" She is answered by a young student who is happy to help. Yes, this is the right MaxiTaxi for the monastery, it will leave shortly[68] when the driver returns. Looking at the people onboard it would appear that this service is much more than just a visitor's bus up to the monastery but a transport link to further up the valley.

2.50 RON and we are on board, the driver hardly acknowledging us before just throwing the notes we have paid with onto the dashboard. As we leave I get a phone call from the Scout party who are currently in Bucharest. It is rather confused, but the upshot is that one of the Explorers' passports is still in the room safe after the rest of the party have left. I suggest that if they miss the flight then they could head north and meet up with us.[69] Next to me an elderly lady makes the sign of the cross as we head up the road, we think that this is as we drive past a church although as we head into the first bend we wonder whether it's because she has been with this driver before.

Reach the monastery to find it surprisingly quiet, although it is early in the morning so maybe it gets busier in the afternoon. It is definitely a much more tranquil place than Bran. There are lots of small stalls lining the route up to the entrance selling various pieces of religious memorabilia. There are also some very welcome well maintained public toilets.

---

[68] We never did discover what time the MaxiCab were supposed to leave.
[69] The problem appears to have been that the battery for the safe had gone dead and the 'emergency override' button would not work. This meant that one member of the trip couldn't get to the airport until someone with power tools turned up and drilled everything out. They made it to the airport with minutes to spare.

We pay to enter the inner courtyard where the monastery is (presumably the wall pre-dates the commercialisation of the area but acts very well to stop anyone just taking pictures without contributing). At the far end is the new monastery and whilst we see no monks the well tendered allotments indicates that they have been working hard. The courtyard is extremely spacious with several small shrines that people are visiting and laying flowers. Our first port of call is to what we think was the bell tower which we climb using some of the steepest, narrowest steps that I have ever come across with the ones on the top section being just wide enough to squeeze through with me having to remove the water bottle from the side of my rucsac as it made me too wide (I wonder how thin the monks were). The narrowness also means that there is no space for a hand rail or rope and I start to wonder who signed off the risk assessment!

The views from the top make the perilous climb worth it as we have a great panoramic view of, not only the courtyard, but also up the valley. As we look over, beyond the entrance and the relatively empty car park, we see that there is a large village on the other side of the road that, for some reason, is shielded from view by a large wall.

Down from the tower and sheltering under my umbrella we make our way over to the painted monastery itself. The lower sections of the outer walls are, as you would expect, faded due to their exposure to the elements but the upper sections (which are protected by the roof) are still quite clear. Restoration work is taking place throughout the building with the entrance being heavily scaffolded, although looking at the number of people working on it and the size of the building it is obviously going to take some time. Inside, where you cannot take photographs, is spectacular following the recently completed renovation with the success of the work being made more obvious by the before and after photographs. Many years burning incense and candles in the small nooks of the building had certainly taken their toll and we wonder whether they now refrain from this practise.

Back outside we tour the stalls and contemplate purchasing a painted egg but after much discussion we think its unlikely that it would get back in one piece and wonder if we will be able to get one towards the end of the trip[70]. Now one of our regular challenges, where does the bus go from? We have a look around where we were dropped off and find what appears to be a bus stop (although no time table) so wait. After ten minutes H is getting twitchy as we have seen no vehicles, of any sort, and she starts to try and work out how we can get to Gura H[71]. Then we discover why there is no traffic as a hearse pulls into view at the church just up the road. It looks as if this has slowed everything down and our MaxiTaxi appears from the queue behind it.

On arrival in Gura H the driver spectacularly dumps the vehicle into a pot hole which is in the gutter, it's not really a crash but you wouldn't have been happy if it was your car. A nasty scraping sound comes from its underside of the vehicle as we get off and head out in search of soup – sadly no local cafes appear to be selling such exotic dishes and we end up on the front terrace of the Best Western where we have a choice of a full three course lunch or lemonade, soup and coffee! Soup is exactly what is required. Then log onto the

---

[70] We do!
[71] H is not good at waiting or queuing

wifi to find out how to get from where we are to the Manastirea Voronet which is down the road from our accommodation. We ask the waitress who is desperate to try out her English on us only to be told that there is "no machine". Initially this confuses us until we realise she means that there is no MaxiTaxi, presumably because it is the end of the valley.

As we are at the Best Western there is a taxi rank straight outside so we head off in the direction of the Voronet, once more the driver seems somewhat reluctant to use the meter and we are not sure if he is trying to rip us off or whether just sloppy management of his time. Seatbelts firmly clasped (again the main clip is hidden under the seat cover so we are hanging on) and we set off at speed disproving my earlier theory that the large roundabout slows traffic down. Past the Carmen Silvae, onto a short section of track (where the tarmac stops and then starts again several times) and then safely deposited outside the monastery. Once more the driver feels that they should finish with a flurry and we arrive in a cloud of dust.

The wall around the monastery is even more substantial than the one we saw earlier and, due to the fact that it is built on a slight rise, means that you cannot even see the roof from outside. We have been pre-warned that they have a "no shorts" policy and so I slip on my long trousers whilst others in the queue try and work out what they can do to get in. The answer awaits them at the pay booth where they are offered a pair of rather unflattering overtrousers, similar items are offered for anyone with a strappy top. On the sign in five languages (Romanian, French, Italian, German and English) it says "We thank you for paying respect to us by respecting yourself!" in capital letters, although the quote in Romanian is in a nice fluid script.

Through a narrow archway we reach a bottleneck caused by them trying to put the pay booth and the official souvenir shop in the same place. Admittedly the claustrophobia of this means that the sight of the monastery in the courtyard is made more spectacular as the view opens up and it is certainly breath taking. Around the edge of the courtyard is what appears to be accommodation, presumably for the nuns and monks. This area is very nicely taped off with Romanian ribbon making it look almost inviting rather than prohibitive. The outside of Voronet is much better preserved than Humor and the pictures much clearer. A large group is being shown around by one of the nuns who is explaining, in detail, the significance of pictures. We try and listen in but as she is speaking Romanian we miss out on much (all) of it. As they reach the back of the building where there is a large paved area the party, that has been having the tour, form up into ranks and burst into, choral, song. We find a bench and take it all in, H with a tear in her eye, it is real lump in your throat stuff. The singing finishes as quickly as it had started, there is a polite round of applause and they continue with their tour. We follow them into the main building and are treated, once more, to choral music (are they a choir on tour who are singing for their entry fee?). The acoustics are excellent but, as we are warned by a sign, we are not allowed to film them and so the moment is lost. They leave and we are back to inspecting the outside and its paintings.

On our way out of the complex, as the bottleneck is more navigable, we have a chance to inspect the small shop selling all sorts of religious memorabilia. Some seem a little strange (rosary beads in the Romanian colours), some more normal (small models of the chapel) and then the very local (pieces of painted wood that seem to suggest that they were taken from a larger piece that was a copy of the paintings on the church!).

Outside I change out of my long trousers and we set off through the many tourist stalls that line the route away from the entrance. Whilst there are many items that we quite like the idea of getting, such as an excellent wooden serving platter, we have to face the reality that we are one week into a four week trip where we have to carry everything with us.

Decide to walk back to the hotel using a combination of Google Maps, dead reckoning (we know it's down the valley, next to the river) and bravado as navigational tools and set off trying to follow the river. Initially this proves extremely easy with a well maintained road/track taking us exactly where we want to be but we are then faced with a *to cross or not to cross the river* dilemma. Knowing that the hotel is on the left hand side of the river we decide to stay on that side *just in case*, rather than what looks like a nicer route on the far bank. We are now taken back through lots of small farmsteads in various stages of repair/rebuilding/neglect but everyone we meet is very friendly and we have lots of waves and "hello"s. Obviously its only English people who wander the back streets, on the outskirts, of Gura. Sadly, in keeping with many waterways in Romania, the stream is awash with plastic bottles and other jetsam that has been washed down.

As we near the hotel and the main road the number of new build properties starts to increase and we wonder how easy it is to commute out of here to larger towns, such as Suceava. Our *commute,* however, is now to the west as we start to look at crossing over the Borsec Gap[72] towards Cluj. But what we do need are some hills to wander around in.

Back in the room and on one of the balconies, we spread out the map and try and work out what our next move was. Much internet searching then ensues and we decide to head for Vatra Dornei, which is not only on the way to Cluj but also does have some hills above it (although the internet is very vague on walks near there). Book in at a low price hotel

---

[72] The Borsec Gap is a phrase we invent in 2016 when we were trying to head west-east from Sighisoara but found a gap in the train service near Borsec. The only way to get past it would be with your own transport as the train/bus service there was very vague. Fortunately, this year, we are north of Borsec and passage from east to west does seem manageable.

for three nights, the idea being that we can leave some gear there overnight if we head off without feeling bad about paying a high price. Now that's decided we head down to the restaurant to see what is on offer today, I go for the Outlaw's Stew that H had yesterday whilst she has something chickeny with a lovely white wine sauce together with more pickles. All of this is washed down with a very drinkable bottle of the local white wine. Once more the hotel gets full marks for the quality of the food.

Our packing takes an unusual turn as we realise that our rucsacs have remained, mainly packed from when we arrived and so its just a scoop up of what we have washed, a quick repack and we are ready.

Watch the last hour of the remake of the Thomas Crown Affair and I'm reminded what a good soundtrack it had, apart from the new version of *Windmills of Your Mind* which lets it down.

Tuesday 8th August – an awful night's sleep constantly interrupted by dreams of being unprepared for the first day of school![73] I am wide awake at 7.20 and catch the end of the World Service broadcast and its transfer to Radio 4 (its 5.20 at home). Lovely to hear Kathy Clugston's voice followed by Louise Lear and the Shipping Forecast. H starts to stir as I am in the shower and, after being presented with her first coffee of the day, suggests that we catch the earlier, 9.14, train. This speeds up our packing and we are paying (674 RON total) then ordering our taxi by 8.10. Bid farewell to

---

[73] Standard dream for teachers apparently. After about ten years of teaching you only start to worry if you don't have them.

our hosts and are heading for the station by 8.20 (possibly our earliest start).

As I previously stated (if you missed it then go back a few pages) Gura has at least two stations (possibly more) and we ask the driver for the wrong one. When we realise and tell him he, simply, does a U turn on the main strip. There is much sounding of horns and gesticulating from other drivers but our man doesn't seem the slightest bit perturbed, in fact he appears to have enjoyed it! We are at the station with plenty of time to get the tickets. Or at least we would be if there was someone at the *Casa*. What we were witnessing was a real life version of the phrase "The lights are on but there's no one at home!" – there is even a cup of coffee behind the screen, although we cannot tell if it is still hot. Check the obvious problems; Is it a Sunday? Is it out of hours? Are there only English people queuing? With the answer to all of these being no we conclude that they have just wandered off for a minute or two. Buy a coffee from the Doncafe machine and stay in the queue whilst H wanders off to get something for breakfast.

As stealthily as she had gone the cashier reappears and tickets are purchased (10.20RON each for a 70km journey). Our reserved seats are in Wagon One which, we guess, is at the front. Out on the platform I await H's return, whilst being eyed by the locals as something of an oddity. It is strange but two slightly crazy looking, middle aged English people with large rucsacs is, almost acceptable[74] but one on their own is just a little weird. They look much happier when H joins me. Local people appear to be on their way to

---

[74] It's not.

the work so I can, kind of, understand their confusion at seeing us.

H has food a-plenty, it was the old "not sure what to get so bought lots of things" approach which we are happy with. We notice a subtle plaque on the wall of the station that seems to be significant so we set about trying to translate it. Our initial thought is that it is about the construction of the station and the railway but we soon realise that it is in memory of the almost three thousand Jews (the entire Jewish community) who were transported to Transnistria during the Second World War[75] on 10th October 1941.

According to the arrivals board the train left Iasi at 6am this morning and is currently running on time (much to our surprise). We are even more shocked when it even arrives on time. We clamber aboard the first carriage that we think must be Wagon One only to discover that it is Wagon Five! It would appear that carriages have been picked up en route. There then follows a wander down the train to Wagon One passing, on the way, a large amount of harvested lavender presumably on its way to market. This gives the carriage a lovely fragrance. We 'overshoot' our *Miss Marple* carriage and realise that we cannot turn around in the corridor due to the size of our rucsacs. We back up and in doing so I almost squash a small child who, somehow, manages to squeeze past us. Rucsacs are stowed on the overhead shelves and we start to work out who our companions are.

---

[75] This was under the dictatorship of Ion Antonescu. After the War the survivors, believed to be around five hundred, all emigrated to Israel.

Straight across from us is a passenger who is on his phone throughout the entire journey chatting away, his arms bear witness to some heavy tattooing many of which look very amateurish and faded. Next to him is a rather smartly dressed gentleman who has a moustache that you would give body parts for. Would guess that he is, relatively, wealthy as he was drinking Schweppes Bitter Lemon (not a cheap drink in Romania). The yawning that both of them are doing suggests that they have travelled all the way from Iasi.

The carriage is rather battered but as we are only paying about £5 for a 50 mile journey then we can't really complain. H comments that she would have rather paid more for a little more comfort (first class is not available on this line), at least it's a reasonable temperature to travel in (low to mid 20s).

Moustachioed Man takes out a very well made, cling film wrapped sandwich. Presumably a late breakfast? Whilst he is doing this we notice that he has amazingly large hands but the end of his index finger on his left hand is missing. Wonder how he lost it? Some sort of ritual perhaps? In these Miss Marple carriages it's easy to let your imagination run wild.

Much to our surprise the train is still on time as we arrive in Vatra Dornei and our travel companions both look up and acknowledge our departure, no idea where they are heading for but Mr Moustache has hardly touched his bottle of bitter lemon. As we are leaving I notice that the toilet door is swinging open (probably broken) and that the floor is covered in lavender, presumably to mask the smell and absorb any spillage but it is doing neither. As we try and disembark we are met with the usual scramble of people trying to get on and in the confusion H is almost pushed back on the train, its only when she gets ready to drop the rucsac to me that they realise that if they don't move then they will be crushed by a large Osprey pack. We now discover why the train is still on time; it starts to pull away whilst (1) H is getting off and (2) people are trying to get on. Maybe the timetable doesn't allow for stopping and that pesky embarkation and disembarkation?

Spotting a sign for Tourist Information we decide that we are in need of a map and some entertainment (this is because they usually tell us that we can't go *there*, can't camp *there* etc, only to find out later that they are wrong). Our hearts drop when we walk in due to the lack of any real literature on the area and certainly no maps on show. We find an assistant who has lots of different ideas for hill walking trips out of the town and is happy to help us, especially when we tell him that we don't want to join the masses climbing the highest peak in the area.

"Good", he says, "It's a long walk on a rubbish track!"

Instead he gets out a leaflet style map and suggests a two day route that we would probably enjoy climbing a local hill with great views.

"Where can we camp?", we enquire.

"Anywhere, there's plenty of space on the summit"

So, with the next few days sorted we head for the Maestro Hotel for a coffee. Sitting outside we have a great view, across the town, towards the tree covered hills to the north. To our left is the old casino which is in a state of disrepair and abandonment (apparently it was subject to a considerable amount of looting following the fall of Communism in 1989 with copper pipes etc being removed). The Rough Guide mentions the state of it but nothing could have prepared us for the sorry sight that it has become[76].

Our accommodation is a stones throw from the casino at the Happy Inn, which is an odd name and it takes us a few attempts to work out exactly where it is as there is no road access (it's actually in the middle of a park) and Google Maps just wants to be very vague! Our room isn't ready yet (it is still relatively early) so we leave our gear in the secure room,

---

[76] At the time of writing there is a suggestion that the building is to be renovated and used as a museum.

with a door that looks bomb proof, and head off into the town.

Staying on the same side of the river as hotel we make our way to the bus station and find a large, dusty area with buses in various states parked up (they almost appear to be parked in bays, although there is no sign of any stand numbers and no markings on the ground). Visit the office (hut) to try and work out where we can go to from here but without any real success. Like many bus stations we have visited, for the longer journeys, it does seem a little pot luck. You have to turn up in the morning and see if the bus is going to where you fancy. Still, we know where it is and decide that we will have a look at what may be available, trains here are strictly east-west between, roughly, Cluj and Iasi. Other places served by local lines appear to have no specific timetables, are not marked on the map or, in many cases, have an almost mythical existence.

A little beyond the station is a large supermarket which resembles a barn due to hardly having any windows and poor lighting, wonder if this is a feature to encourage people to buy more? They have also set it out a little like a maze so you can walk down one aisle and then get stuck – very odd. Manage to get some food for the hill trip, our only concern is how much water we can carry (the Tourist Information bloke has marked on the map various streams where we can get water and we hope that they have not dried out). We also treat ourselves to a plastic bottle of some local spirit. It is unclear from the label what flavour it is but when in Rome![77]

---

[77] Its prune flavour and surprisingly drinkable.

A wander through the town reveals many places to eat, although there are too many pizza places for my liking and not enough local food eateries, but I'm sure the same would be said if someone visited most towns in the UK. From here its time to head back to the hotel so we can sort equipment for tomorrow. The room is large and basic but clean. To give an idea of facilities in the room it lists 'carpets' as one of the features. But we have booked it because of the price so we are happy and ignore the damp patch and the non-functioning extractor fan – what do we always say? Oh yes, its all part of the experience! We spend much of the rest of the afternoon washing gear (the colour of the water from washing my shorts is quite scary after only a couple of days wear). I rig up a washing line in the wet room that makes getting in similar to that scene in Entrapment except with more paracord and less laser beam!

We now pack the rucsacs for a two day mountain trip and H comes into her own. As always she is trying to make her rucsac as light as possible. Unlike our eldest son[78] she only adopts two methods; firstly the "Do I need it?" approach. This involved her ditching her iPod if she can use her iPhone. Of course this means me downloading loads of podcasts for her. By doing this she shed quite a bit of weight. Then, secondly and more covertly, it was the very cunning 'what could I get away with putting in Gary's rucsac without him noticing?' approach. So I end up with the whole of the tent,

---

[78] Tom's approach to lightweight camping (on a mountain marathon) is a wonder to behold. It involves the following questions; Do I need it? Do I really need it? If I don't take it will I be uncomfortable? If I don't take it will I die? On the Original Mountain Marathons I did with him there was a further one of 'If I don't take it can I use my dad's!'

stove and food. As a concession she does agree to carrying the gas.

On our way out we have a chat with the bloke on reception and our plans for the next few days. He doesn't bat an eyelid at the proposal and informs us that we could have put our spare gear in the safe room rather than booking the room but thanks us for doing so.

Our search for food (non-pizza) takes us to the other side of the casino into what appears to be the more upmarket area of town. Whilst I am not wearing a tie I do look reasonably smart so think I can get away with it! The restaurant is attached to what appears to be the smartest hotel in town and, judging by its age, would guess that it was one of those that used to house the rich and famous when they visited the casino. It's a lovely summer's evening so we sit outside. This gives us the additional benefit of being able to watch the people who are heading to the park to promenade.

H has a chicken and mushroom dish similar to the one she had had in Gura H and whilst it is nice it does not match up to the previous one (and is a little salty). I notice a local (Bucovinan) Speciality. This was basically lots of fatty bits of pork, some sausage, polenta and (of course) a fried egg. A Cuic each and we look up to the hill that we are climbing tomorrow[79]. Food completed and H decides that she would like a gin and tonic. Another challenge has been set as we try to match up our English menu with the Romanian one so that the waitress can understand us. Pictures and

---

[79] In actual fact we look at a much closer hill than the one we are to climb but we didn't realize it at the time.

descriptions are matched up and the order is successfully made. During the trip H has started making a list of gins that she would like to sample and so now does a little research into the cost of many of them, this passes the time as we have the usual delay waiting for the bill.

Everything completed we walk over to the river to watch some people on a zip wire flying across it, whilst we assume that it is part of an organised activity the lack of people supervising it suggests otherwise. Then it's a walk back up towards the Happy Inn pausing for an ice cream at one of the many kiosks and to watch the people who come down to the park during the summer months to promenade up and down. Lovely evening for it.

Back to the room for an early night.

Wednesday 9th August – poor night's sleep as there is no air conditioning to regulate the temperature and the location of the hotel, in the woods, means that having the windows open isn't really an option as the mosquitoes fly in.

Our first morning task is to look at the water situation. We each have a one litre bottle but have been told that there is limited water on the hill as several streams have dried up and so we will need to carry more – we have been left a two litre bottle of sparkling water so decide to risk that in the hope that there will be some streams or springs as we ascend and promise ourselves that we will keep them topped up.

Try out the shower in the wet room and H promptly floods it the whole area. The flooding is shortly followed by her usual rant about what she doesn't like about them (wet rooms) and why we aren't going to have one at home (I wasn't aware we were going to have one anyway but there you go).

CNN on the television reveals to us that Glen Campbell has passed away and has some very nice tributes to him – sadly on my phone all I have is By The Time We Get To Phoenix so play that[80].

Through our skylight type window we get the impression that it has clouded over during the night and so may be a little cooler on the hill than we expect. Head out of the Happy Inn about 9 explaining to the receptionist where we are going and when we should be back. She explains how the side door works if we decide to come back this evening/in the early hours of tomorrow. Next stop is the supermarket (the one set out like a maze) to get some bread and cheese. I am left with the rucsacs whilst H does this task and I set out working how the coffee machine works.

Our initial concerns (about finding the start of the path) are soon forgotten as we head off on the clearly signed blue and white path. This takes us up a very well laid out track where we look for a signpost to send us up onto the ridge to our right. This is where it all starts to go wrong as the signs just stop. We come across a post that appears to be some sort of marker but, as it is covered in barbed wire, we conclude that it has been moved from elsewhere to repair this fence! We are joined by a dog that appears to have more idea about where to go than we do and then find some locals who, in

---

[80] Not sure why I have any Glen Campbell songs on my iPhone and certainly confused as to why I should have that one.

response to "do you know where the path is?" merely point up the hill. Leave H, the rucsacs and the dog and walk up the track to find some sort of landmark so we can try and orientate ourselves with the sketch map[81] that we have. I come across some farm buildings that are marked on the map but none of the suggested paths are obvious on the ground. At least this gives us an idea of where we are and where we need to be.

Back with H, who has now changed into her hiking boots[82] and she thinks that she has found a route up onto the ridge. Its not marked on the map but it is in the right direction (i.e. up) and so we start a long ascending traverse that soon turns into what appears to be a quad track before finally disappearing! Above us we spot a ledge that, when we reach it, discover a further track which we follow into the woods. All this time we are followed by the dog that has befriended us and is making easy work of the path. Once more the path ends but this time we are in the middle of a large plantation with lots of fallen down trees on a very steep slope. With little choice we just turn and start to head up scrambling as we go. Our four legged chum is having the time of his life rounding us up, then running ahead, then dropping back etc.

An hour later we reach the edge of the trees. Ahead of us is the top of the spur, a large, almost alpine, meadow. The altimeter tells us that we have climbed around a thousand feet. It has taken us around three hours to cover what we expected to do in one but at least, we think, we are in the right area. A small copse offers us some shade and also a

---

[81] This makes it sound a lot grander than it really is.
[82] To rest her ankle she had walked in this far in her sandals.

blue and white path sign. We look round expecting to see an obvious way up, maybe even a signpost, but nothing. As we are on the spur we at least know that we need to follow this until we meet the main ridge and set off in the direction of the arrow. Four hundred metres later and the path is suggesting that we head down through the trees. Once more I go and scout ahead but discover that the path peters out not far from where is enters the forest. H suggests that we climb to the ridge line again and continue following that, something that our four legged friend is happy with. The views in all directions are excellent (although ahead of us the summit does look a very long way away).

We join a substantial path which looks as if four wheeled drive vehicles have driven up here (there are a couple of cabanas up here so presumably supply vehicles). One is going in the right direction so we are happy that it will take us where we want to be. The track is broken up with lots of puddles. As we walk past one of them H stops and points at something in the road. There, in the soft mud are, clearly, bear tracks that appear to be fresh![83]

A long pause follows and we carry out a quick risk assessment; we are in classic bear country whichever way we go, but its the middle of the day so it is unlikely that the bear will be out hunting. Also the prints are going across our path, rather than along it. Eventually we convince ourselves that we'll be ok and decide to carry on, but not before taking lots of photographs of it using my boot to add scale........after all, they are only prints!

---

[83] By comparing the size on the photo (using my boot for scale) and that of a stuffed bear later in the trip we conclude that this was the print of the adult bear.

We carry on along the track making quite slow progress due to the heat (its around 2pm). Then, without warning, the dog starts barking wildly and dashes into the trees to the left of the path. This is really strange as, previously, it has not left our side and remained very calm. The barking continues getting more frenetic. As we approach the bend a bear runs across the track, about 15 yards ahead, into the vegetation on the other side. The dog is absolutely howling and seems to be seeing it off (although not actually chasing it). We stop dead in our tracks. There is a bear in the area....an actual bear[84] - THIS IS NOT A DRILL! The dog calms down wanders over to us and sits down suggesting that we are now safe, although knowing how fast a bear can run I'm not sure how safe, safe is.

Adrenalin is pumping and our pulses are off the scale. Now is the time to make a rational, calculated decision about whether we carry on up or drop down and we are not really in the correct mental state to do so. We keep asking each other rhetorical questions like are there more bears further on? It is unlikely that the one we have encountered is on its own. Looking at the map it is unclear how much further the forested area goes on for but what we do know is that we don't want to have wasted the climb that we have already done. We decide to carry on, the dog appears to agree with our decision.

---

[84] Later in the trip we realise, having compared the size of the print with a stuffed bear in Bucharest, that the print was from a fully grown bear. We believe that what we saw was only a cub (although it was big enough!).

A four wheel drive, which looks like it has seen better days, drives passed us heading in the other direction and, once more, the dog starts barking. We look around checking that the bear isn't using the diesel engine as cover for stalking us. Eventually we come out of the trees and have a great view looking towards a monastery. To our surprise there is a large farmstead/cabana here, presumably this is where the vehicle has come from. So we open the gate and enter Cabana Gigi Ursus. Its quite busy as this seems to be the high point for many of the walkers coming up from Piatra Neamt or one of the other settlements further up the valley. The dog uses this opportunity to go and make friends with everyone who is here.

"Your dog is very friendly", says a local.
"Its not our dog!" we reply.

We have a choice of several different types of Fanta. Many of them strange colours and flavours, so we play it safe and go for orange. Of course there is no diet or sugar free option! With the dog out of earshot we discuss our position. We are on a hillside in Northern Romania with a dog that isn't ours and are going to descend to a different valley that will put it well away from its home. Its not an abandoned dog as it has a tag on its ear so we must look at getting it back to the valley we have come up from. To add to the mix we are camping tonight and have no extra food to feed it. We order soup and get chatting to the cabana owner about our encounter with the bear, she is quite giddy as we recount the story and then gets positively excited when we ask if the cabana is named after the bears. No, her name is Ursus. She then gets very giggly about whether she should adopt the bear! We explain the dog predicament to her. Her mum is going to drive down to the valley in the morning on business so could take the dog down then but how to stop if following us?

"Leave it with me" she says, waving her finger in the air as if it was a wand.

From here we estimate another four hours to the top and with a sunset time of 8.30pm we should be ok for great views. They do not have running water at the cabana and so, after being given excellent directions, H goes and fills the water bottles up at a spring near the monastery, of course followed by the dog!

Soup arrives just after she has returned and with the dog curled up under our table the owner explains a plan that she has for our four legged friend. As the dog is following H then if she walks through the house then it will follow, the dog will then be distracted by her children whilst H sneaks out through the back door onto the track. At first this seems a little harsh but it offers the best solution[85]. With food finished we say farewell to our travelling companion and H leads him through to the house – we feel like we are on the set of the Littlest Hobo as we set off up the track. The lack of howling from the dog suggests that it was happy playing with the children. Immediately we are back in the trees and are glad that we didn't take what the bloke in the Tourist Information had called the boring long path as this one is proving to be both without much effort! I can only describe it as walking through Kielder Forest but with less people, in

---

[85] The more we thought about this plan afterwards the more we thought how well put together it was. As if it was a regular issue with this dog!

fact the only people we see are some Germans who were picking fruit just up from the cabanna. We mention about the bear and they seem suitably impressed although one of them comments that its on their way down.

A sign points the way saying two and a half hours to the summit and through a clearing we can see a large white cross which we think may indicate the highest point. Many of the paths have been re-routed due to the tree felling that has taken place (we are concerned that this may be part of the illegal logging that we heard about on the World Service as many of the trees appear to have been felled and then left). At least the path changes have resulted in more blue and white markings appearing. As we take a minute a large pine cone strikes the top of H's rucsac, a few inches forward and it would have hit her on the head and could have caused some damage[86]. We conclude its one of the many black squirrels that we have seen running around. This we take as a hint to move and continue on the track before they throw any more. In the middle of this woodland we come across a short, steep section of very muddy track. As we look at the slope a, large hare/small chamois rushes across our path. A minute later we realise that it was a lynx as it darts off up the track and out of sight.

We keep climbing on a rough track and at the top of the slope we are out of the trees and into a large alpine meadow. A sign says one hour to the top and we now have an excellent view of the cross and, near it, what appears to be a silver box shelter. Nothing is marked on the map but its shininess suggests that it may be quite new. H tells me to go on at my own pace and then come back down to collect her rucsac. Pulling ahead I soon come across two teenager girls and an adult, called Arthur (Polish so pronounced Artur). He is very impressed with the size of our rucsacs and that we have walked all the way up. Whilst I am talking to them H catches me up and then we realise why he is so impressed – its because he has driven up! We walk round the corner to find Arthur's Jeep nicely parked up on the col below the top, this was the silver shelter that we could see. We leave our rucsacs by the Jeep and head off up to the cross where there is a plaque marking the Latitude (47.26058) and the Longitude (25.29045), the place (Vf. Giumalau) and the altitude (1858m) just so we know we are not lost. It's a little after 5pm, we have been on the go since 9am and climbed from near sea level.

---

[86] No jokes please.

Walk back down to our packs and the Jeep where Art, who taught himself to speak English (and does it very well) offers us some proper coffee. Be rude not to accept and then, having been offered chairs, sit down for a chat. Like me he enjoys endurance biking, unlike me he has an engine on his and we discuss the craziness of both forms of the sport. He explains that his brother is even better and has competed in the Paris-Dakar where he was part of the support team. His wife is currently ill in hospital with a throat problem and whilst she is convalescing he thought he would take the girls camping (one is their daughter and the other is her best friend). They have driven all the way from near Warsaw. So now it is our turn to ask the age old question "Why Romania?" his answer is far better than ours, "We had our honeymoon here". They are all hoping to continue down to the Danube Delta depending on how soon his wife is better.

Like old friends we exchange stories of our travels, him recalling the problems he faced travelling inside the Eastern Bloc pre 1989 and us about our desire to do so before the Wall came down. As we start comparing plans we hear the roar of diesel engines coming towards us and, from the trees, emerge three very battered 4X4s that are heading for the top. They pause and wave as they go past and Art recognises them, "I met them yesterday, they are crazzeee!", he emphasises the 'eee' at the end as if to make his point clear. They spend a little time on the top before turning round and dropping down to our col where one of the cars stops to talk, the passengers have clearly been drinking (and maybe the driver?) and we are handed a bottle of Honey Jack Daniels that everyone is having a drink out of. We all cheer and, having shaken hands with everybody, they disappear off down the hillside and we watch their headlights disappear into the trees (where they stop for some time, it is unclear if they have had an accident or just paused for a minute, maybe they met the bear?).

Back at the col Art gives out some chilled beers! Seems very odd, wild camping up here with pasta on the boil whilst Team Jeep are gathering wood for a small campfire on the other side from us – we are invited over but decide its been too long a day and, as the sun sets, we climb into our sleeping bags.

Thursday 10ᵗʰ August – sleep well despite the fact that because of the slope, the sleeping bags and the sleeping mats we keep ending up at the bottom of the tent and then have to reposition ourselves back into a sleeping position, effectively by *swimming* back up to the entrance.

Art and the two girls (who when they find out our surname is Bacon find it really amusing) have spent the night sleeping out on a groundsheet using a large inflatable baffle to stop them rolling down the hillside. We are all treated to a spectacular cloud inversion and whilst Art puts the coffee on again we chat about what we do in the 'real' world or more to the point H and Art start comparing sporting injuries. Art is a physiotherapist and starts giving H tips on what she can do about her knee as well as telling her about his brother's badly dislocated shoulder from an enduro motorbike accident.

Breakfast on bread, cheese and sausage plus another Polish Coffee from the back of the Jeep. Art is waiting for a phone call regarding when his wife (Julie) will be released, if it is today then he will head back to town. If not then they are going to head along the ridge and do another wild camp tonight. We pack everything away, say our farewells and head off down the track to hit the Piatra Neamt road to the east of the town where, we hope, we can get a bus back. Do we know that there is a bus? No, as always, it's merely a suggestion that there might be but that's as close to a plan as we have.

As we leave and head down to the main path junction below the col we are met by a strange sight. By the path there is a car that wasn't there last night. It's not a 4x4 but a 'normal' saloon car (a Dacia in the style of a 1970's Simca) and it is parked very well, rather then being abandoned. Surely it doesn't have the clearance to get up the track that we walked up? We look around the hillside and see the owners who are out picking berries (H points out that they are using special scoops to collect them[87]). By the car is a footpath sign indicating its 20 minutes to the cabana, and so 30 minutes later we get there. Or at least we arrive at a building that may, or may not, have been a cabanna but now it looks like it has gone several rounds with Mike Tyson. There is a wind turbine that seems incapable of turning as most of its internals are hanging out and there is a lot of string wrapped round it. The creeking and banging door makes us wonder if this is the Romanian version of the Bates Motel. To one side there is a secure padlocked door that appears to belong to the mountain rescue (there is a large

---

[87] She knows things like this!

sign on the door) and we wonder whether this is only used during the ski season.

We don't stop and, taking a right turn, continue down the track. We are soon overtaken by the Dacia, which has five people in it, and appears to be driven mainly by gravity. The occupants wave at us wildly and we wonder if the Jack Daniels has been doing the rounds of the car! Shortly after the Jeep comes into view, it appears that Julie is going to be released and they are going to pick her up and head down to the Danube (we get the impression that Art doesn't want to waste any more time). Once more we are alone on the hill.

Twenty minutes later and we reach a spring where Art and the girls are, filling up their water tanks. We too top up our depleted bottles and carry on down leaving the Poles to keep filling up, joking that we will see them again soon! Five minutes later the Jeep comes flying past us, pausing only for the girls to give us enthusiastic handshakes before it disappears in a cloud of dust.

We are now faced with a very long walk out in the heat, which is similar to the one we had last year going into Simon. There are, however, two significant differences; firstly there is plenty of daylight (this is a good thing) and secondly we have no map (this is a bad thing). We do have the Tourist Information map but over the last couple of days we have realised that, at best, it is vague and, at worst, it is downright dangerous. We are, therefore, relying heavily on the signs on the trees and there is nothing wrong with this if they are regular. Sadly they are not and we spend a lot of time wondering if we are on the right route. As we are walking down a valley our main fear is that we will miss a turn off or take a turn off that we don't want. Our hope is that this valley, with a widening stream, will lead down to the main road into Piatra.

We lunch by the side of the road in a small patch of shade (a repeat of breakfast as we use up the sausage, cheese etc). The heat is getting oppressive and lacking the breeze that we had yesterday we are both starting to wilt. We both have sunburn, H on her arms, me on my hands and both of us on our legs and this is after ladling on lots of sun cream. Fed and watered we re-commence the long walk out eventually reaching two buildings which are, sort of, marked on the map. More importantly we think it marks the top of the track that will lead to the main road. One of the buildings looks as if it has been abandoned mid-build (not unusual in Romania) whilst the other looks as if it is falling down at a similar rate due to neglect. Possibly now only used by local shepherds as temporary winter accommodation. Straight opposite the two buildings, standing on its own, away from anything, is a small doorless shed, that contains a toilet. Oddly, to say that someone has taken the door, it still has a toilet seat and is functional, ie it flushes. As we explore the track going down we notice that half way up one of the electricity poles (which presumably have taken power to the half built/half fallen down structures we have just passed) is a large, lever style, on-off switch that we conclude must cut off the power to the upper end of the valley. More importantly it confirms that we are approaching civilisation.

Next up is a sign saying 1.4km to *Forester* but as we have no idea where or what that is all we can do is speculate that this is near the road and, hopefully, a bus stop! The poor phone signal means that we have no Google Maps either, although the ever helpful altimeter does speculate that we are at a height of 132metres below sea level![88]

Finally we come in sight of some, inhabited, farm buildings and, as if to confirm that we are ok, a phone signal. This puts us 1km from the road (it also gives us an altitude of 750metres). We pass *Forester*, it's a very large sawmill with lots of people milling around totally ignoring Health & Safety regulations whilst the machines churn out lots of planks (in their defence I see no one wearing sandals).

Finally we get to the road where there is a small settlement that appears to exist purely because of the sawmill. At the café/general store we dump our rucsacs outside and treat ourselves to a Sprite for H and Chiu Radler for me. Sit in the, relative, shade of a very battered umbrella to work out our next move. As always we attract odd looks from those around us. This time our company is made up of truckers and loggers all of whom must be struggling in this heat. Suitably refreshed we ask after the bus back to Piatra and are informed that, " Yes, the bus does go past here" and we are pointed in the direction of what looks like a mid-1970s bus stop just over the bridge from the café.

Its 4.15 as we shelter in the shade of the bus stop. We ask an elderly local when the next bus is and she says "five" and waves a handful of digits at us. After 20 minutes we realise that she was indicating five o'clock and H tries, unsuccessfully to hitch. For the first time the bus is on time and we clamber on board. Our driver, Mr Grumpy, demonstrates all of the usual traits that we have become

---

[88] From the map we guess that we are closer to 850metres

accustomed to, by pretending to not know that the bus is going to Piatra Neamt. We are saved, once more, by a teenager who translates for us. Our money is exchanged for tickets and whilst out tickets go safely in our pockets the driver launches the money onto an untidy pile of cash on the dashboard, maybe he is penalised for picking up passengers? Sit towards the back of the bus with our rucsacs on their own seat in front of us as the bus speeds along the road. The only other passenger we pick up on the way is a middle aged man who a carrying a felling axe without a cover on it (no one bats an eyelid).

Now we are customers of the bus station we view the place in a different light and almost understand the parking system (with the non-existant markings). As we always do we thank the driver as we get off in the hope that, next time, he will smile. Now its back to the Happy Inn to chip off two days worth of mud and check for ticks. As we walk through reception we get a thumbs up from the staff, they look surprised that we are alive (maybe they knew about the bear?) - then its up to Room 11 where H falls asleep for an hour before its time to change and head out for dinner (whilst the Happy Inn does food it mainly appears to be pizza etc hence us eating away from the hotel).

The gear that we have left to dry whilst we have been in the hills can now be packed away and we start to make piles of gear ready for moving on tomorrow.

Showered and changed we head over towards the Hotel Ceahlau for dinner, going via the mineral water building where we can partake of the local water. This is all round the back of the casino, which looks in an even worse state from this angle with broken down fencing which would offer little resistance to any would be thief!

Whilst H goes for pork in a whisky sauce I have pork in a cheese sauce (pig meat is very popular in this part of Romania). Mine comes with two lots of carbohydrates in the form of polenta and chips which sit on the plate scowling at each other over the pork then almost taunting me to overdose on carbs! The hotel is trying very hard to attract the Western visitors so, once more, there is no local beer and I am left with Staropramen. Its an odd clientele staying here and I wonder how many of them are seeing the country or just seeing the inside of a hotel. Someone decides that they want to put the football on the large screen and we use this as our opportunity to leave so H asks for the bill. The waitress is thrown by our request to pay by cash rather than card – it appears that no one pays by cash anymore and she scuttles back inside to sort the change (despite our insistence that it doesn't matter). The restaurant, relatively quiet when we arrived, is now filling up and one of the staff is rushing around frantically putting out reserved notices on several tables as more and more people start to hover near the entrance. As we get up to leave our table is quickly grabbed, I wonder if its for the football or the food?

Walking back passed the front of the casino we have a much closer look at it and wonder if it would have fallen into such neglect had it been in Iasi, Brasov or Bucharest. Birds are nesting in it and it looks as if much of the roof lead has been removed. Whilst it is fenced off there are obvious signs that people have been going in, for whatever reason, and I have little doubt that we could have done without much effort[89].

From here its another stop off at the Betty's Ice stand where H has a Magnum style chocolate ice cream whilst I go for a very creamy vanilla ice cream with added cream (I can almost feel my arteries hardening as I dig into it). We now, once more, join the people of Piatra as they take in the park on a balmy summers evening. It seems a lifetime away from where we were yesterday and we wonder how far towards the Danube Art got after picking his wife up.

As we pause H checks on Trip Advisor and finds that the park gets something of a kicking from many visitors with some very poor reviews. Presumably these are from visitors who expected something much more spectacular than just a park as it is certainly a magnet for people of all ages. A little like you would find in many French towns there is a group of elderly men gathered around a battered table playing chess, around them are several rows of spectators watching, and commenting, on every move. There is such structure and hierarchy to this with the youngest on the outside looking in, trying to view the skills of their elders on the hallowed table.

The youngest children in the park are happily playing hopscotch on a very neatly drawn out grid that they have done in chalk (we wouldn't have been surprised if they have used a ruler, it is that well done). Looking around we can see no obvious graffiti and guess that as the local community are using the park a lot then it is self-policed. It is very much a place to relax and take it all in. Couples of all ages are either walking hand in hand around the grounds or are snuggling up next to each other on one of the many benches.

---

[89] Investigation later reveals that much of the interior is propped up. Little of the ornate interior remains.

Down one edge of the park, near the rather faded band stand, are several small kiosks selling a variety of local products, including a few that are selling fur products of numerous designs and would guess that it is cold here in the winter[90]. After saying that some of the colours that the fur has been dyed make you wonder how cold it would have to go before I'd wear some of them (think pink, purple or luminous green).

Time to head back up the hill to the Happy Inn where, on the bar terrace, everything appears to be just getting going. I suppose that some people will have taken Friday off and are making a long weekend of it. We head back to Room 11 where H packs some gear into dry bags so it will be easier to pack in the morning.

Tonight's film is a Steven Seagal one where he is saving the world, or a Native American Reservation, or something like that. Stayed with it for all of twenty minutes before putting the radio on (it was no Under Siege!). H just falls asleep.

Friday 11th August – once more its time to move on. Piatra Neamt is a lovely little town and is exactly what we have needed (even with the bear) The way our plan is rolling out we are now going to be heading, initially, into more familiar territory over to the west of the country.

H's muscles are stiff and cramping up this morning and I think that the 8 mile downhill walk out yesterday has taken its toll on her knees as her movement isn't as fluid as it

---

[90] Average January low is -5 degrees.

normally is. All gear is wedged back in the rucsacs ready for today's train travel. Despite the fact that we have been here for a few days and the rucsacs have been totally emptied (for the hill) we manage this in a quick time, leave our key with reception and head out in search of breakfast.

The sun is shining as we walk past the fur shop (the only one of the concessions that is open) where H sneaks a quick picture of the goods on show and I notice a clear sign that says that all the furs are from a known source, what this exactly means I'm not sure. The rest of the park is very quiet, not even anyone playing chess.

Cross the river to our first port of call, the station for tickets to Cluj. As we are aware of various options to get there I just ask for tickets to Cluj, rather than waving the train app. The cashier taps away on the keyboard in front of her before smiling at me and typing on her calculator and holding it up to me. It reads 11.01, she is telling me the time (she's obviously done this before). I smile back and indicate two, we both laugh at the simplicity of the communication method we are using as she then shows me the price (60 RON) for the trip that will take us over four hours. Tickets bought, we eye up the expensive looking coffee machine that is inside the office, drinks from this are twice as expensive as the ones on the platform and we conclude that this is why it is inside. As we eye up both machines we realise that we have well over an hour to go and can get a real cup of coffee from a real person and still be comfortably back for the train.

So into town we head in search of breakfast and a coffee or two. Quickly find a café that offers 50% of our requirements (no breakfast) so decide to defer food to the mini-market and get the coffees in (did toy briefly with walking back up the hill to the Maestro but had ordered coffee by that point). Whilst waiting for our coffees, and watching the world go by, an elderly gent appears who seems to be trying to sell sharpening stones. Someone buys one so he immediately sits down and orders a beer. Its 9.30 and we don't think that its his first.

Have a wander down onto the main shopping area and come across the war memorial, complete with cannons on either side of it. Next to it is a rather impressive town hall. Many of the buildings in the centre of town appear to be quite old and whilst not totally devoid of concrete it looks as if most of the Communist Concrete has been kept on the outskirts, perhaps a deliberate effort to keep it desirable to tourists? In the middle of the shopping area we find a minimarket with a frontage of a little over 3 metres wide but which goes back many tens of metres according to H (I am left outside to watch the rucsacs). Breakfast and travel food purchased and we go to the platform to sample some of the Nescafe sponsored, machine dispensed coffee – it is horrible!

Despite this (and probably because of its cheapness) it does a steady trade as the platform gets busier and busier. Like many of the stations in Romania the one in Piatra has access from various directions and you don't have to go through the main building, so no one does! This results in people coming in from the other side and just walking across the tracks to get to the platform and, my favourite, a bloke walking along the tracks from some distance away, without a care in the world, looking like a scene from Lawrence of Arabia as he emerges from the heat of the desert (although in this case its from the direction of the supermarket).

We realise that it's the Bank Holiday weekend so we are certainly not alone for our trip over to Cluj and the packed platform certainly confirms this. Most of the passengers look similar in their appearance and luggage but one man stands out, it takes me ages to realise that its not his bright yellow Stihl braces holding up his trousers. It's the chainsaw that he has slung over his shoulder! And before you ask, no the blade was not covered, he obviously wanted to get straight at it if required. His travelling companion, who looked much less suspicious is carrying a large holdall. Obviously conscious of the possible health and safety issues they go over to the other platform and wait for the train to arrive.

We need Wagon 2 and get ready for the usual "Guess the train number" challenge. It therefore comes are something of a surprise to find them clearly marked (starting with 5 at the engine end) and we soon find ourselves safely positioned in a Miss Marple carriage together with a father and son duo. The first section of the journey, out of Piatra, takes us through lots of trees, then a few tunnels. We were hoping to get some good views of the mountains but are sadly disappointed.

Then, as we were expecting at some point on the trip, the train breaks down! To be perfectly honest we were expecting it sooner as the train was getting slower and slower and we were already 30 minutes behind schedule. A new train appears (from where we do not know) and we wonder if they were expecting this to happen and so had brought up a replacement ready. Needless to say that, due to years of practice, they are swapped over very quickly and we are on our way again. The guard appears, too late to apologise for the train breaking but in time to ask if the air conditioning is working. Our companions indicate that it is not, mainly by gesturing their hands in a flapping motion. The guard makes a very impressive gurning face and, ignoring the problem that it is very hot, shrugs his shoulders and wanders off. A visit to the toilets on the train brings up an odd surprise as we find that the toilet seat appears to have been set for someone well over six feet in height, I guess that they were just trying to get it fitted quickly!

The train continues at a now brisk pace as the driver tries to make up time.

H asks the younger of the two Romanians if this train has broken down before. The reply is succinct, well thought out and highly accurate, "Of course, it's Romania!" He then asks THE question and when we reply, waxing lyrically about the countryside etc, he says he must take a fresh look at it.

We finally arrive in Cluj about an hour late, this means that our companions won't get to their destination until well after 11pm (assuming the new train keeps going) so we wish them good luck for the rest of their trip. Then its out onto the platform. A quick glance around tells us that we are back in heavily populated Romania, i.e. lots of concrete, and whilst the station building itself is nice there is the standard issue apartment blocks across from it (and a very Communist signal box just down the line).

So, to find the hotel, we crank up Google Maps. We have specifically chosen the hotel as it is in easy walking distance of the station (so we are not taxi dependant) and are therefore surprised when it gives a distance of over a mile to walk. Five minutes into the walk and we realise that Google has defaulted to travel by car and we are following the one way system along a very straight road that appears to be heading straight for the centre. System reset and five minutes later we are in the reception area of the hotel. It is all based around a courtyard (which is open to the elements) with the rooms on different levels above it so from each level you can look down to the main dining areas. The stairs are quite narrow and dark (the automatic lights seem less than keen to come on and only do as you are past them). With rucsacs this is made even more tricky. Eventually reach our room (208) and walk in. It is on two levels with the sleeping area on a mezzanine floor (or shelf) up some steps. There is a barrier around it but I'm sure that falling off is a possibility with a little effort! We also have two TVs, although the one on the shelf resembles an old portable TV that many people have still got in their spare rooms[91].

Once the tour of the room is complete there are jobs to be done and we fully utilise the bath by washing lots of gear in it before stringing it out around the room. Again we are surprise by the amount of gunge and generally grey water that comes out. As our plans are, still, very vague from here we have to try and clean stuff when we can just in case we make a dash somewhere. We have no food and neither of us fancy going out for dinner so I am given a list and set off to try and find a supermarket. Downstairs a party is starting to take shape. H falls asleep!

---

[91] Or, until recently, cluttering up my garage.

Standing outside of the hotel I try and work our where I am. To the right is the road to the railway station. We walked in this way and I can't remember seeing any large shops in that direction. So, I type into Google Maps "Lidl" and set off. We have read that Cluj has lots of great architecture but soon discover that this must refer to the centre of the town as the section I am in is standard issue grey concrete tenements. Most of these have large air conditioning units bolted on the outside with water dripping from them onto the pavement. What I also notice is that whilst many of the roads have been built on a grid system, and so are easy to navigate down, little thought has been given to where the old roads intersect with them (normally where there is a bridge or similar) and so large, manic junctions have evolved (similar to the one outside the station in Iasi). For a pedestrian they are bad enough, as you try and work out how to get from one side to the other (like playing human chess). I can only imagine how bad they are for the drivers.

Spot a Carrefour and abandon trying to find Lidl in favour of a small, subterranean shop beneath a multi-storey car park. Rather disappointingly I have found possibly the smallest supermarket in Romania. In their defence they have managed to wedge in lots of aisles, although in doing so they have made them very narrow (trolleys not recommended). Still it has the basics that we need and 88RON gets us two bottles of wine (one red and one white), beer, bitter lemon, an assortment of meats and cheeses and bread. Have a steady walk back to the hotel noticing the floodlit cross on the hill above the town and pausing to admire the complex nature of the bridge over the river[92].

---

[92] It appears that, rather than build a new bridge when they wanted to

Now to remember the room number. I know it's on the second floor and the windows are closed, this narrows it down but I still make a bad guess and open the door to 205! Immediately I realise my error and utter, in my best French (?), "Excusez-moi...." and close the door. As I head over to 208 I wonder why my default setting had been French. Safely back in the, correct, room I check the thermometer and even with the air conditioning unit chugging away its showing 31°. Its Friday evening and we are a long way from home, so what to do but listen to Radio 4's Last Words[93], Glenn Campbell has died this week and I wonder if my father was first in the line with a request[94].

By 10pm we are on the shelf Kindles out (having abandoned any ideas of watching the small TV). We leave the bathroom light on so navigation down the stairs is much easier.

Saturday 12th August – the not so glorious 12th if you're a grouse, good luck my feathered friends and happy birthday to our friend Pete.

As previously stated we are sleeping on a shelf. It is much more glamorous than that but it is still a shelf. On the plus side the shelf is much higher than the window and so we are not woken by light streaming in. We reminisce about the

---

widen it, they just bolted some bits on the side. When it needed extending again then another piece was bolted on etc.

[93] Last Words is an obituary show that profiles recently deceased people of note (I won't insult them by calling them celebrities).

[94] My father was a Country and Western music fan and whilst he never bought a Stetson, went to the Grand Ol' Opry or similar he was a truck driver.

last time we slept on a shelf (the Alps in 1983) and how much more comfortable this one is[95]. Although, even with the lack of air-con back then, it was much cooler. By the side of the door we notice a large sign that warns against opening the door while the air conditioning is on. Whilst this is probably more about saving power the unit does make a clunking sound when the door is opened as if to warn us about killing the planet.

Best night's sleep of the trip so far, slept straight through. I think that this was down to two factors; firstly we were all in from yesterday's travel and secondly our reluctance to try and attempt the stairs down to the toilet in the half light. The morning starts with Tony Blackburn on the radio via iPlayer and the news that, once more, the US and North Korea are on the brink of war. On yes and one of the UKIP candidates is standing on an anti-Islamic ticket[96]. Glad we are well out of the way.

Breakfast is included in the price so we head down to the courtyard area where the tables are tucked away to the sides for a non-buffet breakfast. This is quite unusual on this trip as most places offer a large spread that you can gorge through. H goes with the omelette, and surprises the waitress by asking for mushrooms, whilst I go for the rather homely sounding Full English Breakfast, with beans. Both are delicious, although mine would have been better listed

---

[95] The shelf in question was in an abandon cable car station where we had had to hack out ice before propping up the shelf with our ice axes!
[96] This is how it is written in my diary. The UKIP person was Anne Marie Waters (https://www.telegraph.co.uk/news/2017/08/12/anti-islam-campaigner-approved-candidate-ukip-leadership-election/) on the nature of the conflict between N Korea and the US.

as a variation on a Full English Breakfast. The breakfast conversation now moves on from sleeping on shelves to where we are going to visit in Cluj and where are our travels taking us next (we are looking at heading south from here and wonder if a stop off in Zarnest is possible[97]). We order more coffee but it never arrives.

In the meantime, where in Cluj must we go? I contact a Twitter friend who is originally from Cluj but now lives in the UK and she suggests the Botanical Gardens, a "must see", the brewery and, oddly, the cemetery. So these are added to the list, alongside finding the Tourist Information Office. On leaving the hotel we have to leave our keys at reception (I suppose a simple way to tell who is in and out) and are asked, "Do you want your room cleaning?" I resist the temptation to warn them that there is lots of gear drying out in there and just answer "...errr....yes!". As we have now started a conversation I ask, "Do you have a map of Cluj?".

The reply is not what I expect, "Do we have a map of Cluj?" said in a way as if she wants to say is "Do WE have a map of Cluj?" as if to indicate that they have one but we can't have it. My confusion is corrected as she presents me with a very simple map torn from a large desk blotter size pad. She marks on points of interest and then apologises for the, probable, state of the Central Park area following last weekend's festival (it was the Untold Festival that kept us out of Cluj last year when we ended up staying in Turda), "There may still be some teenagers there!".

---

[97] Where we had visited with the Scouts in 2015.

We set off into the heat using the well-rehearsed, 'I think it's over there' method of navigation to try and find the centre (whilst making a note of where the hotel is) make our way towards the supermarket that I went to last night. Now there is a large outdoor market where everyone seems to be selling their wares. There doesn't seem to be any system, the locals just turn up and sell. Lots of different fruit and veg on offer as well as many wood worked items. Looks as if it's a locals market, for locals. From here we can see the roof of one of the major churches so, crossing a very complex road junction, we head towards it. This brings us into the central area of the town and the architecture immediately improves. Behind us are the concrete constructions of the Communist era whilst ahead of us are the older buildings from the 1800s.

We make a beeline for the Orthodox Cathedral which is set in its own area, the Avram Iancu Square, and in doing so manage to hurt my foot when I trip and stumble over a large heap of dried concrete. Not sure why this is there as there are no signs of any building work being carried out in the near vicinity. Inside the cathedral is very cool and spacious. Our initial thought that the building is really old is quickly corrected when we discover that the main piece of it is only around one hundred years old. At the far end is a very impressive chandelier that was presented to the cathedral by Carol the First and is currently being held off the floor by the some rather substantial scaffolding which is a work of art in itself. We wonder if the scaffolding is also holding the main dome in position. In the church we are joined by the usual mix of; (1) the devout, who are here for the daily prayers, (2) the young pilgrims who appear to have been brought here by their parents to, as the bar manager in

Piatra put it, 'kiss the walls' and (3) the visitors (who are very much in the minority). Now, this is where I always get a little twitchy. If I go into a church that requests that you wear long trousers or cover your shoulders then I have no issue with it, similarly if it says no photographs then I don't even pause before putting the camera away. But I think that a natural default setting should be to dress with a certain level of decency. With this in mind I am quite shocked by the shortness of a dress worn by one of the female visitors (I have longer t shirts!), surely common decency should be maintained? Rant over.

Tour done we walk back into the heat of the square and find some shade from which to admire the statue of Avram Iancu with the Cathedral beyond. Whilst we sit trying to work out the best way to get from here to somewhere else in the shade a policeman arrives on a Segway and does a very impressive lap of the statue before moving on[98]. On the opposite side of the square, and over a busy road, from the Cathedral is the equally impressive Opera House/Theatre. Outside is a group of tourist signs pointing off indicating how far it is to various landmarks and when we see it mentions the Tourist Information Office we, once more, feel like we should try again with our love/hate relationship with them. Our journey is interrupted as we pass a café and decide to pop in for a lemonade. The layout of the café is not dissimilar to our hotel and fortunately has an excellent shaded spot in the courtyard where we look at the vast array of different lemonades on offer, these include two different sorts of forest fruit (according to Google Translate!).

---

[98] We see him later moving a street vendor on for presumably not having the correct permit. He manages to do this without stepping off the machine which is very impressive.

Fortunately we have a waitress who is more than willing to translate and she explains that one is normal forest fruit but the other is rose. A split decision as H has the forest fruit (real one) and I have the mint, once more the lemonade doesn't disappoint and I wonder whether "Lemonades of Romania" would make a good blog or even another book.

The travels of the last week, being to the north of the country have meant that certain noises have become more foreign than others and one of these is that of aeroplanes. Cluj airport is obviously quite close to the centre and we are getting them both arriving and departing. Using an app we discover that the WizzAir plane we see is heading for Doncaster. To add to the 'who is flying in' mystery a German family sit down at the next table who appear to have just arrived.

Lemonade consumed we set off again on, what is turning into, the wild goose chase to find the Tourist Information Office. The signs appear to have been carefully positioned so that you have to do a tour of the centre in order to find it, thus seeing all the sights and so negating the requirement for the office (genius). Finally, more by luck than judgement, we come across the Office. The map (and signs) not only put it on the wrong side of the road but on the wrong road entirely, I reassure myself that this is because it has recently moved[99].

We ask after getting to the hills to the north of Turda (west of here and beyond where we had explored in 2016). Yes, there is a bus that leaves Cluj every day at 3pm. His answer

---

[99] Don't know if it has.

is said with such confidence (about the existence of the bus) that we are sure that he is making it up, no one at the Tourist Information Office has ever made such a statement with such precision! We now have a possible area to aim for so we ask the killer question, "Can we get maps of the area?"

There is a long pause as he looks around the Office, "We do not have them......no.....but", our hearts lift, "......but they do sell maps next door, or there is another one across the road". Before we can say or do anything he marks them on our map (which has been resting on his desk) and then says, "Here is the mountain shop, I'm sure they will sell you one" (I'm tempted to say that we are not looking to buy a mountain but feel that the joke will be lost). Of course the shop closes at 2pm (its now 1.45) and doesn't open on a Sunday.

Next door doesn't have a map of the area we need, although it does sell some maps (mainly of places outside Romania). We head up towards the Cathedral, passing on the way a great fountain area in which loads of children are playing and getting soaked. As we watch a police car pulls up and a, rather overweight, policeman goes over to talk to the families, not sure what about as the children carry on playing in the water. Across the top end of the square is what appears to be a service road so vehicles such as ambulances can short cut the one way system. At one end of this 'rat run' is a parked another police car, this one with its blue lights flashing away, presumably to stop people just driving that way. Leaning on the car is its driver who appears to wish that he wasn't stuck here acting as a mobile bollard.

Two more bookshops visited but still have no map, although we are offered a 1:200,000 map that appears to cover most of the country and the shop owner is surprised when we reject it (maps are not yet fully understood in Romania).

Across the square and into the Cathedral which is free of charge (a sign says donations welcome so we donate). A very impressive pulpit and knave but, sadly, the walls have fallen victim to the 'Paint the Fresco' brigade that did the same to the Church on the Hill in Sighisoara. Some paint and plaster has been removed to show what lies beneath but it is unclear if this is an ongoing project. Overall the Cathedral falls in to that category of a building that is more impressive from the outside than it is on the inside. This is especially true when viewed with the Matias Rex Statue in the foreground.

"Its going to rain!" says my ever vigilant companion as the clouds start to roll in and the temperature drops. Working on the 'Better Safe Than Sorry' maxim we decide to head to the history museum as it will be indoors, on the way buying a salami and cheese turnover from a street baker.

Initially we think that we are the only people in the building as we appear to be being followed everywhere by the staff but then realise that, as its quiet, a member of staff is following every party! On entry we glance at the list of museum rules (of which there are many), my favourite being that you cannot ride a bike around it. This is made even funnier by the fact that the rules are posted halfway up some very steep stairs. The rules, together with the information leaflet, gives us the impression that they subscribe to the Google Translate, which we love. The museum is well laid out and gives the impression that a lot of thought has gone into what is displayed and what information given, considering much of the history of Romania is very, very complex[100].

We complete the tour and as we try and locate the toilets the human barometer points out of the window saying "Told ya!" and there is a very heavy rainstorm that lasts all of fifteen minutes, but manages to flood sections of the road outside as the drains struggle to cope. It cools down, slightly.

Our trusty, free, tourist map takes another battering as we go rather astray trying to head towards the cemetery (another must see). The problem is that the 'helpful' pictures on the map obscure the details that are required to navigate! Eventually we come across a useful landmark (the river) and are able to work out where we are (a long way from where we wanted to be but good for what we were wanting to do).

Amidst the chaos of Cluj we spot our first two prostitutes of trip, one outside the Post Office in a little black number, red high heels and a lot of stuffing on her upper torso. She is gesturing wildly at the traffic going past as if wanting the cars to stop on a road that would have caused an accident. The second was slumped on a step at the entrance to a courtyard nearby.

---

[100] Whilst Romania, as an entity, has only been around for about a hundred years it had previously been ruled by various countries. Look it up, its fascinating.

H, still recovering from the long, hot descent into Piatra Neamt requests a stop so we sit on a park bench where she, almost immediately, falls asleep. I sit and watch the world go by as the weather starts to brighten up again. Romanian Afternoon Society is out and about in droves this Saturday afternoon in a way very similar to what we found in Piatra Neamt with people promenading up and down the park. Thirty minutes of battery charging (snoring and dribbling) later and H is ready to carry on so, arm in arm, we join the rest of society strolling through towards the boating lake and casino. Its been a week since the Festival and, whilst there is some evidence of it, most of the wreckage has obviously been moved. All that is left now are a few bits of fencing and some trodden down grass. I'm sure that had the weather not been so kind then it would have been a little more battered. Off the path, but still in plain sight, we spy some people with hammocks strung up in between the trees and wonder if this is standard practice. Looks like a great way to spend the afternoon.

Expecting to see a casino in a similar state to that in Piatra Neamt we are extremely surprised to find a very well finished, very white building which even has a red carpet leading up to it. Its now owned by the local council and no longer a casino. Instead it appears to be the definitive wedding venue in the area. There also appears to be some sort of event going on inside. Outside the cream of Cluj's youth are all having their photographs taken for their portfolios and there are lots of them all gathered around the various photographers. I shoulder my camera with pride and adopt a 'I'd rather be in a war zone taking photos than do that' stance[101]. Around the front of the casino there were what appeared to be a series of marble fountains (but it they turn out to be painted stone, perhaps concrete) many of which were actually functioning. The good people of Cluj obviously believe in civic pride judging from the amount that has been spent on the area around the park. Moving on from the casino is a large boating lake with a lot of swans on it and some pedaloes for hire. At the other side is a rather fancy looking restaurant/hotel/bar which we decide needs our business and sit outside for a drink, looking at the pedaloes and wondering if we should go for it. A strawberry lemonade (for H) and a frappe for me later and our thoughts drift towards what we should do next and where should we eat? The menu here looks great but as we look through the guide book etc a little voice shouts out a better idea, "Let's go to the brewery!". We have no idea of its location but the Rough Guide raves about it so that is our next challenge[102]. We have a few options about how to get there, it is marked on our unreliable map (which is slowly disintegrating anyway due to overuse), there is a description of sorts in the Rough Guide and there is a small map also in the book. We take the logical step and crank up Google Maps (remembering to select walking) and, once more, launch off into the afternoon. The description that it is on the outskirts of the town is a little misleading, on the outskirts of the centre yes. As always I make a mental note to contact the guide[103].

---

[101] I have no idea what that really looks like but I certainly pointed at the Duck Tape that was on my camera holding it together (since fixed).
[102] What we don't know is that about 200 yards away is a bar owned by the brewery that does excellent food.
[103] As always I didn't.

As we approach the brewery we realise that we are near the cemetery that we were trying to get to earlier. Outside the bar area is very busy so we head inside where we are immediately met by a large carved wooden bear. It is cool, they are playing 80's music and there is a large chandelier made of beer bottles. Looks like a good choice of eating venues. The menu is not extensive and this makes choosing food much easier[104]. I go with salmon penne whilst H goes with the chicken in cheese with olives. We ask after a plain green side salad (not on the menu), the waitress doesn't bat an eyelid, "If you want, I can make, what would you like on it?" H asks for olives on it, obviously suffering from an olive deficiency and, again, no problem. What excellent service.

A large Ursus goes down well. Its been a long time since I'd had what I thought was called a stein but is called a masse[105]. Remembering the advice we got in Bucharest last year we go for unfiltered. The bar area is very large with many different nooks and whilst it appears to be quiet at the moment most of the tables are reserved, presumably for the post football crowd (there is a television in the corner showing a game, although there appears to be less people in the stadium than in the bar!). The toilets are tucked away at the back of the building and in order to get there you have to walk past the old brewing equipment which is all on display behind large glass panels. Various signs are advertising live events that happen here and we make a mental note to return. As the place starts to fill up, we head back into town,

---

[104] I have reached an age where I would rather have a more limited choice so I can choose more easily.
[105] Or a one litre bucket!

pausing only to have our photograph taken with the wooden bear!

Decide to head up the hill that I saw yesterday evening, the one with the cross on it. How to get there poses another challenge, as we know that there is a river between us and it, but where to cross? Using a combination of the map and the 'it's over there' approach we make our way through a rather salubrious part of town[106] and end up at the stadium. Here a game of football has either just finished or is about to finish. I step up the ramp to try and get a photograph looking towards the pitch but am stopped almost immediately by a security guard who appears out of nowhere. We cross the river at a very pleasant footbridge (Podul Elisabeta[107]) and then follow a very busy main road before finding where a footpath heads up the hillside towards the cross. This starts off as a rough track before joining a very well made (but not well maintained) series of steps up to the cross and the Hotel Belvedere. The views are spectacular and whilst we don't get a sunset we do get a lovely glow over the city. This spot is a little like the park in Piatra where the locals have gathered at the end of the day. Quite peaceful considering that the Hotel Belvedere, that dominates the skyline, was once the home of the Securitate[108].

On the way down we consider stopping at a café which has a sign saying "We serve everything!" but decide that weird

---

[106] We discover later that there is a much easier way to get down to the river which avoids this area.
[107] Built in 1901 by the army and currently the victim of the dreaded lock fastening craze.
[108] The Securitate was the Romanian State Police – worth researching if you are interested in Romanian history.

food can wait until later in the trip and make our way through the back streets towards the hotel. En route coming across an intercom on a nearby building that, for some reason attracts our attention. Firstly because one button is for a Peter Andrei and secondly a sign for Toth Dezideriu Pesti Exotici (apparently Toth Dezideriu Exotic Fishes). After due consideration we decide not to see what sort of exotic fish are available and head back to the hotel.

We enter reception through the courtyard area.

"Are you wanting to book in?" asks the Receptionist who we had spoken to earlier.

"No, we are guests, can we have the key for Room 208 please", I reply.

"Oh, are you a guest?"

"Yes", obviously sounding a little puzzled.

"What room number?"

"208"

"Oh yes", key is handed over.

Now I am pretty sure that there aren't that many English people who she has booked in over the last 24 hours so it does seem an odd conversation. Still, we have our key and head back to the room where H tries to sort out a heat rash that she has developed on her ankle, this involves ice and witch-hazel.

No late night film as its way past our bed time, we climb onto the shelf and snuggle down.

Sunday 13th August – H sleeps like a log and hardly moves all night. On the other hand I struggle to sleep, probably because of how quiet the hotel is having been used to the noise. On the plus side I finally get to hear the full podcast about North Korea that I have been trying to listen to for a couple of days. I am also finding the bed a little on the large side, I think that I've played squash in smaller areas.

Around 7 I get up and creep down the stairs from the shelf letting H slumber on. Put the World Service on for an update and am surprised to get a text from some friends in the UK who are in the Lake District hoping for a mountain sunrise. Settle down and try and catch up on a bit more of my book. Eventually H starts to come out of hibernation and I am dispatched to get the, all important, breakfast tokens. I give them my room number, it is logged and the number of tokens I am allowed is checked. I am presented with the tokens before I offer my thumb print or passport as further proof of who I am. Walking round to the dining area I find H has had to *negotiate* with the staff to get in as "You don't have a ticket!" appears to be their mantra. Make a mental note that, as far as breakfast is concerned, we have to be joined at the hip!

Safely settled we feast on meats, cheese and the English Breakfast (a different variation today). We manage this by splitting our individual choices between the two of us – much to the amusement (confusion) of the staff. Make a mental note that H took more egg than me. Two cups of coffee today and so we conclude that the waitress is happier. On another table we think that we hear some English voices, our first in two weeks, but resist the temptation to go over and talk to them. H's sluggishness appears to improve after the second cup of coffee.

Having a late start and later finish appears to be the Romanian way and so we decide to have a couple of hours in the room reading and sorting gear (another thought that we have is that we can get a batch of washing done in the morning and it will dry whilst we are out so it will be ready for packing for tomorrow). H is currently murdering (no pun intended) a Val McDermid Novel whilst I have just finished rereading Newby's A Short Walk in the Hindu Kush and moved onto Blitzed, a rather odd piece of work about the use of Meth Amphetamines in Nazi Germany and WW2[109].

Whilst the sun is high in the sky the cloud cover means that the temperature is much more tolerable as we make our way to reception and go through the usual booking out procedure. Our plan is to go to the Botanical Gardens by taxi (its at the opposite end of the town) and then walk back. The receptionist indicates that the taxi will be with us in three minutes, wildly waving three fingers at us to confirm it. We are only down the road from the station so are not surprised at the speed at which it arrives. What we are surprised at is the position of the driver's seat which is so reclined that he is almost horizontal with his head effectively in H's lap (I'm sure its not a standard seat). Whilst H is looking at the driver trying to avoid a drive by shooting I am

---

[109] Blitzed: Drugs in Nazi Germany by Norman Ohler

wrestling with my seatbelt trying to locate and fasten it, this task takes me most of the journey.

When we see the entrance to the Gardens we say to the driver, "anywhere here is ok". An instruction that he appears to ignore as he just drives through the gate and we are dropped off on what is the entrance path right outside the ticket office. 13 RON for a dash across Cluj but that's what you get from the one way system.

The Gardens themselves offer a mix similar to Iasi but in a smaller area, although it does score extra marks as it has a lot more signs in English. The first glasshouses that we come across are almost empty, and locked, and it takes us some time to work out that this is where many of the larger potted plants are wheeled in winter (the trollies etc. give it away). We follow the logical route that is, sort of, arrowed and head to the Japanese Garden which is in a hollow. Getting there we have followed a middle aged couple where her outfit was, to say the least, eclectic; it consists of a light 'floaty' top (sensible in the heat), a pair of cycling-type shorts (again practical, although the stripes were not very flattering) and some very high wedged shoes (not at all practical on these paths and I find myself with one hand on the first aid kit, 'just in case'). As it happens we take the right hand path and they take the left so our first aid skills are not called upon.

We drop down to the edge of the Japanese pond and cross it via a bridge that is made up of a few paving slabs which have been balanced on some rocks in the water. It looks less than safe but we cross it anyway. From the other bank we can see the wooden bridge on which lots of people are having their photographs taken. As expected we arrive at exactly the moment that the Mongol Hordes come flying down to take pictures on it as well. What we now witness is one of the best examples of speed photography ever as they all work with each other to take the maximum number of photos of themselves, themselves with friend(s), group shots and so on. They then get twitchy when they can't get a photo of just the bridge.

As quickly as they have arrived they have moved on and are heading towards the main glasshouses further on in the Gardens. This gives us long enough to appreciate the calm and serenity of the area before the next coach party arrives. We head off to continue with our first aid stalking of the couple we had seen previously although we soon overtake them and arrive at some very impressive buildings whilst they are still struggling on the last uphill section. Outside the buildings is a very large tree that appears to have fallen some time ago and has now become a feature. People are queueing to have their photographs taken inside the hollowed out section and so we have to do the same. Again, this is an exercise in speed photography as people sort out their own system of queueing so we all get a chance. Inside the glasshouses, which are well worth the entry fee on their own, we are treated to the sight of huge lily pads complete with a photo by the door of a child sitting on one. Having had it hot and unpleasant outside we are now transported to a tropical climate where we are expecting all sorts of exotic animals to drop from the trees onto us. Next we go through into what could be called the Banana House due to the numerous huge banana plants that dominate it. H offers to take a photo of a couple who are struggling to take a selfie (and not a selfie stick in sight).

Outside we can breathe again, although it's still hot and we pause on a bench and find we have an unexpected cabaret of a girl jumping off a log whilst someone is trying to take a photo of her. Not sure what they were trying to achieve but they appeared to be enjoying themselves[110]. The Gardens are spread over 14+ hectares and have expanded to fit the

---

[110] I wonder what happens to all of these photos, in days gone by they would have had to pay for the hundreds of shots that subsequently end up on a hard drive somewhere.

area available over the years (they were built in 1920) so we drop down to the stream that goes through the site, noting that it is not possible to get into the Gardens by following the stream as all illegal entrances/exits have gates or similar across them. Turning away from the entrance and climbing up we approach a large, now abandoned, water tower where H manages to persuade me to go the top where the views are excellent, well they would be if it wasn't for all of the trees that are blocking it. On our descent we come across a lad who is, obviously, scared of heights and is being talked up by his friend. I try and reassure him that where he is (with exposed rusting stairs) is the worst bit.

In the area below the towers there are some lovely reclining statues by a water feature and beyond that we go and inspect the kitchen gardens where H is in her element naming all of the crops that are being grown and I am genuinely impressed (although she could have made up half the names and I wouldn't have known!). Beyond the garden is some scrub land and an overgrown fence that appears to be the limit of the Gardens, of course we go and inspect what is on the other side. Unsurprised to find that it is just more scrubland. H finds some plums that are growing wild and declares them delicious. I decline the offer as I wonder what chemicals may have been put on them over the years to control the growth. By this point we have lost what little path we should be following so make our own, rather off piste, route back to the entrance where we find the ice cream stand has just closed (probably run out of ice cream in this heat). Its time to head back and from where we are, as we head back into town, the next logical place to visit is the cemetery as it is 'just around the corner'. Whilst we find it easily enough, getting in is a totally different matter as a large security fence surrounds the grounds and we have to drop right back to the main road and use the main entrance. The steepness of the road makes me wonder how people drive up here in winter[111]. Around the entrance, not surprisingly, there are several funeral directors and florists and, as we arrive it looks as if a funeral has just taken place judging the number of people leaving. To the left of the entrance the foundations for a large office or residential complex are being dug, seems an odd place to position such a building but then land is at a premium in this part of town.

We are immediately stuck by the sheer size of Hajongard Cemetary[112] and its position on the hillside is certainly impressive. The headstones vary from small simple crosses (even some wooden ones) through to mausoleums of varying sizes. On some of the stones there are names of husbands, wives etc with a date of birth but no date of death and we conclude that these are for when they do pass on. Not sure whether we are impressed with their forward planning or thrown by their 'this is where you are going to be buried' approach (I suppose it's one less thing to plan). Making our way back down to the entrance we cannot help but notice a large group of soldiers who appear to be waiting just inside the main gate. Our first thoughts are that they may have been a guard of honour for one of the recently interned, then (as they only seemed to have their normal fatigues on) that they have been escorting someone on a visit here. To be honest they may have just been seeking shade.

---

[111] The idea of a road zig zagging up a hillside seems to have been lost in Romania – if it doesn't go straight up then it's not worth bothering with appears to be the mantra.
[112] We later establish that its about 14 hectares.

Heading back towards the town, in search of food, we walk passed the Catedrala Martirilor si Marturisitorilor which is under construction, and has been for 20+ years. This puts us in sight of the City Walls that we follow through the park and back to the main square where we go into the Rhedey Café[113].

   As we sit down a Maggie Reilly lookalike walks through, prompting H to offer her thought, "Nice hat......probably an arts student!"

5.25pm and outside the weather is starting to close in a little. Tomorrow we are due to move on and H makes an excellent observation, "Where are we going next?". We realise that we have not planned the next stage (other than we are heading south). Whilst we are waiting for our food H looks up the top things that you must do in Romania and it appears that we have ticked most of them off[114]. Our travel discussions are interrupted by our food arriving; chicken in ginger for H and pork with garlic for me, the menu warns of the strength of the garlic sauce and they are not wrong, I suddenly feel safe from vampires for the rest of my life! The Rhedey is not as large inside as you would expect but manages to fool the eye with extensive use of mirrors and excellent lighting. The great design features carry on in the subterranean toilets where water for the sinks just comes out of a pipe from the ceiling, the tap is on the bottom of the sink. Also in the basement appears to be a large entertainment area/night club, although we see no signs for it.

---

[113] The name sign says proudly, 'Established 1995'
[114] I have never liked the 'must do' lists that people put together and dislike the 'must do before you are <insert age here>' even more but at least they can give some suggestions. And don't get me going on Bucket Lists!

Dinner consumed, table cleared and another beer ordered, we get the map out to decide where we should go next and we start to work back in days from the Delta, this is all carefully written out on a serviette as we try and confirm the travel plans in our own minds. Tomorrow we have a long haul down to Brasov, approximately 300kms, from there we hope to grab some time in the mountains near Sinai before heading to the Delta. Or something like that![115] Head back out of the old town, via a small Carrefour and to the hotel where we find a wedding reception is taking place. Music for the early evening is provided by a violinist and a pianist. Later in the evening it becomes a Romanian Singalong, I'm pretty sure that we hear their version of Roll Out The Barrel!

Now we are in the comfort of the room we clear the floor and spread out the map fully. Initial thoughts are that we go to Brasov with a view to trying to get to the valley to the north of Zarnest, although without a map this could be tricky. The other problem we are facing is the lack of maps. Whilst our safety was not exactly compromised on the 'Bear Hike' the tourist leaflet maps are almost useless. Art did recommend an app but it is Android only so that scuppered that plan. Bookings.com is cranked up and we find accommodation near the railway station in Brasov which promises mountain views.

Turn in around 10.30 as the wedding party keeps going.

---

[115] We are now at the point where planning involves looking at when we need to be in Bucharest and working back from that.

Week Three

Monday 14th August – another poor night's sleep. This time caused by the temperature, even with the air conditioning droning away like a jet engine it is still too hot on the shelf, although the bathroom is a little colder and I do wonder if we could take the mattress down there. Ended up listening to the Inquiry Podcasts going back a year.

7.30 and we are up and rucsacs sorted. We forego breakfast as they do not start serving until 8 and this would totally throw our timings. Book out and order a taxi to save a little time. Its only when we get in and set off on the Cluj One Way System that we realise that it would, probably, be quicker to walk.

When we arrived we had taken little notice of the station and the surrounding area so it is all new to us when we get out of the taxi. My favourite is the 'slots' that the taxis have to go into which appear to be made so there are no queue jumpers (similar to Iasi Airport). The state of the walls at either side suggest that there have been many misjudgements! Oddly, no toilets in the station. They are in the underpass outside and are amazingly small.

Manage to sort tickets without any problems even though the microphone system does not appear to be working properly and I find myself saying "pardon" a lot. Fortunately I am served by one of the new breed of cashiers who is nice, helpful and treats me like an eccentric Englishman. For a Monday morning the ticket office, and the station in general, is surprisingly quiet. Ticket in hand we decide to try and find somewhere for breakfast, there is not a café in the station itself[116] so we wander outside and end up in the Station Café which, as you would expect, is a distance from the station itself. Order Espresso Long (big uns) but are served normal size ones, not a problem as it's a pay as you leave and we just wave our little cups. A quick calculation and we realise that it is going to take us about eight hours to cover the 331 km to Brasov (this equates to about 25 mph) so travel food is purchased at another one of those mini-markets that have a small entrance but then go back for 50+ metres. Thinking that its much smaller I offer to stand with the rucsacs and by the time H emerges I have lost feeling in my right foot, on which her rucsac has been balanced.

Back to the platform to wait for the train and we notice a very 1970s building at the far end which looks as if it was built as the control centre for a spaceport or similar (we think it was the signal box). Now it looks abandoned and everything is housed in the main building. H goes to try and get some coffee from the machine (little tip; even though the Nescafe machine is cheaper and carries a known name don't have it. Why? Because the coffee is horrible). She returns a little later with black coffee, "I couldn't work out how to add milk". This is a problem we had in 2016 so got used to it and were just happy to get a drink.

A sign on the platform tries to explain the complexities of the layout of the station and where different trains go from. It also shows the order of the carriages and their numbering. We are in wagon 5 which is separated from the engine by

---

[116] The station at Cluj is really odd as, despite it being quite large, it has neither toilets nor café on site.

wagon 6. Surely it can't be that easy to work out which train it is?

The train pulls in, or at least a bit of it does and we are faced with an engine and two wagons, this is not shown on the diagram. Chaos promptly erupts on the platform with lots of waving and grumping from the locals. We just decide to get on, after all this is our train, going to our destination and we have rucsacs to sit on for eight hours. The fact that it has less than the required number of carriages isn't an issue. As we approach the train another three coaches appear from along the track together with another engine. These are coupled up and we have a complete train (we resist the temptation to ask if they had become uncoupled down the track). So, we now get on the second carriage down from the engine, only to discover that this is number 4! Move onto the next one, which should be 6, to see an electronic sign indicating that it is number 5. Looks as if 6 has gone AWOL but this one is air conditioned, so we do the usual rucsac juggle to stow them on the overhead shelves and settle down for the journey. Map comes out to check where we are and where is Brasov. Plans on revisiting Zarnest are scrapped in favour of dropping down to Sinaia or Busteni and then going into the hills from there.

Opposite us is a man who looks like a young Trevor Horn, he is staring at his iPhone in a way that suggests that he is having a staring competition with someone over Skye. He stays like this for much of the journey.

The journey drags, of course it does, as we have a third of a day stuck in a biscuit tin on wheels looking out at the same agricultural landscape. H is now even happy to get excited when we go past some concrete edifice just to break up the trip. My previous timing calculations start to haunt me as I realise that we are at least 20 minutes behind before we even get to our first stop![117]. This is the area that we were delayed in 2016 (heading for Sibiu) and ended up on a bus with loads of other stranded travellers. The problem appears to be the new high speed track that they are laying from Budapest to Bucharest. I know that it will be all sleek and shiny but I can't help thinking that they should maintain some of this old rolling stock, for nostalgia's sake.

A group of teenagers board the train at Halta Unirea, another station that appears to be have been left over from the Wild West. They are carrying a lot of badminton rackets and a large bag full of shuttlecocks, in fact way too much gear for six of them. Maybe they're a travelling badminton school? The guard has a word with them, what about I'm not sure, but they immediately sit down and go very quiet. Wonder if he threatened them with the bus ride over the tops?

Our route takes us past Sighisoara and then above the Fagaras Valley. Sadly any views of the mountains is cut by a small ridge embankment next to the line. As we are but a lowly Regional train, in order to make way for another train to pass, we pull into a siding that is at a rather jaunty angle. So jaunty in fact that the water bottle, rather unceremoniously, slides across the table and falls onto the floor. The further south we head the more concrete and less greenery we seem to get. Yes, there has been concrete around the places we have been but not quite this amount.

---

[117] From here is goes downhill, that's metaphorically as Brasov is higher than Cluj (340m vs 540m)

So, we are parked up on a siding at a weird angle, the train we have pulled over for has gone through some time ago but there is no sign of us moving (has the driver been thrown off?). We should have been at Sighisoara for 1.45pm. It's now 2.15pm and we are, to all intents and purposes, parked up in a field.

After what seems like an eternity the engine stumbles into life and we set off at the usual leisurely pace that we have come to expect. The next piece of entertainment we get is when the air conditioning breaks down, the guard is summoned and someone explains what has happened. At which point he goes over to a control panel, opens the front and starts to wildly push the buttons. Lots of red lights come on, then go off, then one goes amber but the air conditioning remains broken. We are then treated to a series of waves and hand gestures as he indicates that he is going to go and talk to someone. A minute later he appears, shrugs his shoulders and gestures that it is very broken. At this point he gets some grief from the locals so he resorts to his special back up plan and goes to open the windows. For this he needs a special key that he goes to retrieve, returns to more abuse, opens windows and leaves. H shuffles to the other side of the compartment out of the sun, I just pull my hat over my eyes and go to sleep, only to be awoken by the heat and the feeling of sweat dripping down my back.

Finally we arrive in Brasov about a month behind schedule. On the plus side our journey ends here unlike many others who are carrying on through to Bucharest. Out in the large, very Communist, foyer area we are surprised to see that the windows that they have been working on for two years are finally finished. Oh yes and there is no very smelly man queuing for tickets (see last year's adventures). My phone indicates that our hotel is only 700m away and so we set off up a hill walking through what is typical, near the station, downtrodden, concrete buildings with very odd car parking facilities, ie you appear to just park your car where you want regardless of whether there is a pavement, road junction etc. As we reach the top of the hill we are greeted by a large, new, four star hotel. Can this be right? We have been travelling on a hot train for eight hours, only half with air conditioning. We probably smell. Still nothing ventured.

We go into an immaculate reception area and the best receptionist so far. She is smiley (without being insincere), enthusiastic (without being too much like a children's TV presenter) and friendly (without asking if she can marry one of our sons). On top of that she is not at all fazed by the Newby Cat reference. Fill in the forms, there appear to be more for the posher places, and up to our room. All the time we are aware of the newness of the place and we soon discover that it has only been open a few months. So to the room, where we have; robes, a hairdryer, loads of toiletries and A KETTLE! (the first of the trip). Kettle immediately goes on for a cup of Yorkshire Tea to remind us of home and we take in the mountain views. In reality this means looking between two other buildings that are built close by, and we have a good view into some other people's apartments opposite. Still, mustn't grumble as we've got a KETTLE!! It goes on again this time for a hot chocolate.

We also discover that we have several English language channels on the television, you can tell that we are now back in the more Westernised tourist areas. Channel surfing produces a few surprises and a channel that I'm not sure should be on open access, hope that they get the censorship sorted before families start to book in. Put on BBC World.

The power shower is excellent and hacks off the travel dirt (and smell) – oddly its in a sort of wet room with a door. This means that when you open the door a veritable tidal wave is let loose on the rest of the bathroom. We make a note of this on the feedback sheet. Back down to the dining area where there is no sign that dinner is served so order a taxi and head into town[118].

Brasov, whilst not quite having the splendour of either Iasi or Cluj is certainly a town well worth visiting and this is our third visit in as many years. The main town square is very busy and we find out that tomorrow is St Mary's Day[119] which is a public holiday and so everyone is taking the opportunity to get out. The crowds are really strange after two weeks being in quieter places, although I would guess that other towns are just as busy. A runner goes past us wearing flashing trainers, one orange and one green!

Our tip for places like Brasov has always been to find somewhere away from the main area to eat as, normally, the variety and price of the food is better (even though the people watching isn't as good!). With this in mind we end up at the Ursul Carpathian Restaurant for stuff cabbage leaves, something that we have struggle to get on the trip so far. A carafe of Romanian wine and we review the day. This

---

[118] Turns out that they were not doing dinners until the autumn.
[119] Celebrating the Assumption of St Mary

mainly involves wondering if the wedding party from last night have sobered up yet.

It's getting late and starting to go dark but people are still wandering around the little stalls of the outdoor market which is a hive of activity. We have a browse but, being aware that weight is still an issue, decline the temptation to purchase anything.

The station, and our hotel, are both a long way out of the centre and so we set off to try and get a taxi back. This proves to be no easy feat as we have chosen the time that everyone else is doing the same but discover that, when it comes to taxis, the Romanians can queue very well. We get dropped off at the station so we can have a walk before getting to the hotel and manage to find an open shop for milk so we can have more tea.

Back at the room we phone home to confirm that everything is ok and then get the map out to sort out whether Sinaia or Busceni is going to get a visit.

Tuesday 15th August – we have proper curtains that fulfil their purpose very well as they go all the way to the floor and meet in the middle. This, and the chaos of yesterday, have resulted in a good night's sleep. Whilst we do have BBC World there is no Breakfast so we manage with the news from around the world and a quick trawl around other English language news channels.

Our plan when we arrived yesterday was that we would not unpack our gear so we could get off without any issue this morning. Unfortunately, the hunt for the teabags (due to the excitement of getting a kettle) last night has resulted in gear being strewn everywhere. In fact it looks like we've been burgled! We ignore the mess and go downstairs for breakfast.

Maybe because of the nature of the trip, or the nature of the accommodation we have stayed in, but we have either had no breakfast or a la carte style so it is a delight to find that we have a buffet breakfast here with an excellent spread covering several tables. The room is busy and the only thorn in the side of the waiter is the coffee machine which he points out is new and not working very well. In fact it is working but it seems to decide what sort of coffee to dispense, at what speed it will come out and how much it will dispense. Like a petulant teenager the coffee machine only stops when it has run out of coffee beans and even then it emits a whiney sound that tries to drown out the piano based jazz that is being played over the hotel speakers. We are well and truly full after a mixture of cold and hot breakfast food and head back to the room for a leisurely pack (leisurely as there is no rush for the train and because we are enjoying the air conditioning). Catch up on the world news on CNN in HD as we are pretty sure that we won't get such luxuries in Busceni.

Book out and are asked to leave a "good review" on Trip Advisor – we point out that we already have done. 700metres seems a lot with a big rucsac but it's all downhill so not an issue. Stop off to buy nail scissors but at 20RON we decide that we can manage.

Tickets purchased from a helpful, but grumpy, cashier we realise that we have nothing smaller than a 50RON note (around £10). This causes her to start waving her arms a lot as she would like us to pay the 10.60RON with something smaller. She sighs a lot as she gives us the change. We are very apologetic. With time to kill we head to the shopping centre that is next to the station, separated only by a taxi rank then a large car park. As we walk through the rank, we are approached by one of the drivers who offers to take us wherever we want to go, I point to the shopping centre and say "We're only going there!", which gets a laugh.

I am dumped in the café where last year we killed time waiting for the train to Victoria on our outward journey. It's as empty as it was last year and I wonder how it is still going, on the plus side my phone automatically logs onto the wifi as I order a Mint Frappe to try and cool down (when it arrives I realise that it contains alcohol and its not even noon!). H wanders off to try and get some light trousers that are suitable for the Delta. Some game show plays to itself on the television in the corner (last year it was a weird Woody Harrelson film so a strange Romanian quiz seems reasonable).

The shopping mall is filled with Scouts of various nations (judging from their badges) who also appear to be killing time. H returns without a purchase but with the confidence that she will be able to get something over the next few days. Feeling rather light headed (how much alcohol was in that drink?) we head back to the train station. This involves some fancy footwork across a car park, to avoid being run over, and then through the taxi rank. We pause at a sign next to the parked taxis that advises travellers which ones to take, or more importantly which ones not to take. Oddly the sign is at the opposite end of the way you would approach them from the station and would require a diversion to see it.

"Taxi?", calls a very tall friendly looking driver.
"No thanks we've got a train to catch"
"Are you sure?"
"Don't worry, we'll support your friends at the other end"
"Where are you heading?"
"Busteni"
"No need for train, you go by taxi!", then, "200lei and I take you there". He has a wonderful twinkle in his eye.
"Ha, ha…no!", we all (including the other drivers) have a good laugh at this as we all admire his enterprising approach. It was worth a try but he was charging twenty times more than the train and we already had our tickets.

Platform One is an odd place to get to. We go into the station, down the steps, up some more steps and across the concourse, only to realise that we could have just walked to the left of the station building without going through the main entrance and avoiding the many steps.

The Scouts have gathered on the concourse nearby and the football is out, it looks as if they are in for a long wait. The sensible ones are in the shade. Our train is in so it's all aboard. It's very busy as this is the main one for Bucharest but, as it's a double decker on, we manage to find some seats Any thoughts of stowing the rucsacs on the racks is dismissed early on as they are the smallest, flimsiest ones of the trip so far. Suitable only for a small shoebox and so insubstantial that they, probably, couldn't hold the weight of the shoes in the first place. Rucsacs placed on the seats instead (safer option). As today is the coolest travelling day we have had so far it is only fitting that CSF had made sure that the air conditioning it working overtime keep our legs very cold.

We leave exactly on time (not sure I've ever written that about the Romanian trains) and make good time for the first 30 minutes. This is made much more entertaining as we watch the Scouts try, without any success, to put their rucsacs on the racks.

Then the train stops! Why? We have no idea but its in a similar place to last year (although it is not raining). We can hear the engine still going and the air conditioning is still freezing our feet. We exchange glances with the others in the carriage but no one says anything.

There is a long pause, well a pause of about five minutes, and as quickly as the train has stopped it starts again. Nothing is said. The train carries on making the odd noises and we still have frozen legs.

As the station approaches we don our rucsacs and go to queue to get off. From the number of people waiting it looks as if this is a popular stopping off point with fifty plus wanting to get off and well in excess of a hundred waiting on the station platform to get on. The train grinds to a halt with a reassuring thud and the doors open. Equilibrium is almost immediately established as those on the outside fail to understand that they cannot get on until those getting off get off! A tall bloke in front of us yells "Oi!" to establish some sort of order but it has little effect other than temporarily stalling the invasion. Step forward the ex-Primary Teacher who breaks the chaos by shouting "Excuse me!" then, channelling her inner Alan Whicker, puts her hand forward to part the waves and walks through the now divided group on the platform. It would appear that this turned a lightbulb on in the collective consciousness as we all get off, H giving a thumbs up to her crowd controlling buddies and, in turn, they thanks her for her help.

We are now in Busteni and whilst our friends head to the centre of town (to our left) our accommodation is to the right about three quarters of a mile along the main road (according to Bookings.com) off which all of the town radiates from. It seems much longer than stated on Google maps as we pass first a Lidl, then a monastery and then the town limits! The Conac Bavaria lies just beyond it and is in a German/Austrian style. The owner speaks excellent English having spent six years in the Netherlands before moving back to Romania to run the hotel and explains to us what there is to do in the area. The explanation of why we are booked as Newby Cat is easily accepted although we are then asked "Why Romania....?" which, even though she has waxed lyrical about the area, she struggles to understand.

Having used Bookings.com in 2016 we are surprised with the next issue we face as the deposit for the room has been debited from our Visa card. This is more of an annoyance/inconvenience than anything so we let it pass and make our way up a very narrow staircase, through some very keen fire doors (keen as in we struggled to push them open) and to our room which has a sign on the door saying "A Princess Sleeps Here", which cheers H up. She is also cheered up by the fact that we have a balcony. However, as we are on the front, whilst we do have views of the hills we also have great views, in the foreground, of the road and the railway line (on the plus side the river here is not navigable so there is no freight on it to add to the noise[120]).

With Jaws on the television (followed by Jaws 2) we start to go through the tourist information leaflets that we have picked up from reception about suggested walks and plough through the various websites suggesting what we should see. We have a vague plan of 'let's head to the hills' and with that head back down the road to Lidl to get some supplies for tomorrow. We have also decided that after here we are going to make a push out to the East and the Danube Delta, which will involve an overnighter in Bucharest but that is for another day.

For convenience we decide to eat at the Beer Kellar which is attached to the hotel[121]. We split a Sausage and Bean Stew and a Spicy Meat Stew between the two of us washed down with a Ciuc (sadly it is only in bottles as they have no local beers on draught). The other dinners are a mixed bag of families, couples and a table of very smartly dressed gentleman who appear to be having some sort of business meeting, complete with lots of pieces of paper and waving arms.

Fed and watered and its back to the room to watch TLC, one of the few channels that is in English. Its all about obsessive cleaners and features a woman, who describes herself as a 'full time mum' and spends over forty hours a week cleaning.

---

[120] This is a running joke that we have about street noise following an overnight stay at a campsite in Heidleberg in 1989. This may appear in a future book "Collective Ramblings of a Travelling Yorkshireman"
[121] Judging from the number of evening guests it appears that the restaurant is the main draw here rather than the accommodation.

We also catch up on a couple of episodes of the Archers (the time difference means that we find ourselves targeting where we will be at just after 9pm local time) and then its time to snuggle down hoping that the road/rail noise decreases and that the blindfolds we have make up for the standard issue inadequate curtains.

Wednesday 16th August – even though the curtains don't work (they have the usual gap in the middle and are made of a pale ineffective material), we are on the main road to the north from Bucharest and are a stones throw from the railway line we still sleep surprisingly well, maybe it's the mountain air?

Up early, pack day sacs and down for breakfast at 8 for the first sittings, we are approached by a waitress who says something fast and Romanian to us, H looks up and says "In English?" to which she happily replies "Five minutes" in excellent English (it appears that we are early). She gestures us towards the coffee machine where we encounter a very efficient, relatively quiet service and a substance that is very drinkable. Bookings.com compliments their breakfasts and we have to agree, a large variety of different meats and cheeses on the buffet spread and unlimited refills from the coffee machine, which H enjoys playing with. Nicely fortified, but still a little unsure of where we are heading, we gather our gear and make our way to the reception. All of the routes we are looking at start at the telepherique, we just need to get there. We discuss different possibilities with the manager whilst we wait for the taxi to arrive and our general thought is that we should head towards Mt Omu (a hill that we had planned to visit last year but there was much confusion over whether we could stay at the, small, hut or whether camping was possible).

H gets in the front seat of the taxi and wrestles with her seatbelt whilst pointing out to the driver that she is English and, therefore, always wears a belt. In the back I have no option as the seat belt clips are buried under the seat covers (of which there appear to be several). The driver, kindly, helps H sort out her belt as he pulls away and then answers his phone as well just to prove that he can multi-task. During the journey I would say that the driver did not have at least one hand on the wheel for at least thirty percent of the time. No wonder the windscreen has a crack that gives the impression that he has already knocked someone down.

At speed we make our way down the main strip closely following a motorhome which chooses to do a U-turn. Sadly they choose a point where this is close to impossible and necessitates a three plus point turn which causes lots of angry drivers who have to slow down. The driver of the motorhome does not seem the slightest bit bothered about this and continues on his way north towards Brasov. With the obstruction now removed the taxi is brought back up to ramming speed and we head towards the cable car station.

Similar to most taxi drivers in Romania we are dropped off as close as he can get to where we asked, ie the station. The fact that we are, very much, off road, on a path and two people have to move out of the way merely adds to the adventure and we climb out, coughing, into a large cloud of dust. Our driver, gesturing towards the queue, wishes us luck and disappears off down the hill side scattering people in his wake. We turn and face the queue which is wrapping itself around the building and up the hillside – TripAdvisor points to some times of the day when there is a four hour wait. We felt that our earlier start would avoid this but we start to wonder how long the wait will be and guess it will be well over an hour[122]. Its 9am, the sun is coming out and its starting to warm up.

At least this way it gives us time to plan what we can do. The cost to the top is 35RON, one way. If we want to go over to the next valley (where we had descended to last year) then it's an additional 35RON, again one way. Quick mental calculation and we work out its roughly £30, one way, to the next valley with a similar charge for the return journey as walking back isn't really feasible. A better alternative is cable car up then head up to Mt Omu and the route that we had hoped to do in 2016. From there it looks a, relatively, straight forward (although long) descent back to the village. As the queue come around the front of the station lots of taxi 'chancers' are trying to persuade people to take their taxi around to the next valley, the whole trip will take four hours and there is even a 'formal contract', although what that really means we have no idea. I explain that we are heading into the mountains and, whilst his route does look nice, it has no relevance to us. We are thanked for our time and, together with his nicely laminated sheet, he moves onto the next people no doubt saying 'formal contract' a lot!

9.30am comes and goes and H strikes up a conversation with a lady behind us as soon as they both realise that they speak English. They (she has a husband and four children in tow) are from Israel and are staying at Predeal having flown into Cluj and then driven round. They drove the Transfagaras

---

[122] It is worth noting here that H doesn't do queuing very well, if at all!

but it was thick cloud and so they are hoping to see the mountains on their return journey. The family intend going up, having a wander around the Sphinx Rocks then catch the cable car back down. Remembering the queues last year I wonder how much of their day out will be spent queueing compared to the length of time they will spend doing things.

10.30am and we are finally inside the cable car station where it is a lot cooler. From inside we can see that the queue has extended considerably and we can understand where the estimated four hour queue has come from. Looking at the parched field we realise that many of these people will be queueing during the heat of the day. Hopefully the water seller will do deliveries. As we get in the final section of the queue to board the car I put on my "How to survive a trip in a cable car by self hypnosis" tape[123] and concentrate on my breathing.

Stepping into the car immediately makes me think that the time I've spent waiting would have been better spent climbing the hillside but with the calming voice talking through my headphones I grab hold of the pole in the middle and try not to cry. In my defence I do manage the first section with my eyes open only closing them as we do the longer spans where H informs me there were some long drops which I wouldn't have liked! We pass over the hut where Sleepless in Seattle was playing last year and then are just skimming the tops of the trees as we follow the path up towards the rock formations.

---

[123] Can't remember what its called but its something like that.

The first things we see as we emerge from the cable car station are a group of stalls selling various pieces of religious memorabilia, obviously to persuade people that it is safe to catch the car down if you have a new crucifix. More people appear to be getting off here rather than carrying on into the next valley. We find a spot away from the crowds to reshuffle our gear as it is a little cooler here than it was in the valley before having a brief wander around the Sphinx and the other rocks. Here we leave the main path, and crowds, and start to head north towards Omu.

The first section gives us wonderful views over to the route that we followed in 2016 up the Valley of the Bears over towards Simon and Bran (although we notice on the map that this year it's called the Gorge of the Bears). We can even see the refuge that we stopped at for lunch, although it's a long way off. The only people we see on this section are a family who appear to have befriended a guardian sheep dog (that we try and stay well clear of). To our right we have a view of the large transmitter that dominates the Sinai Valley (or the rocket as we refer to it). This view gives us the first clue as to the weather changes that are blowing over as cloud slowly envelope it and the surrounding area. Jackets are put on and we change from summer to warm hats as the wind starts to increase[124]. Paths now start to go off at different angles and we aim for a slightly higher ridge route to the left. Unfortunately, soon after starting up this, the wind increases to the point that we are forced to drop back down to the normal route which skirts around the edge of the rock face with a steep slope below us. This route does give us the added interest of a shepherd out with his flock.

---

[124] We are still wearing shorts.

He is wearing camouflage clothing, wellington boots and is blending in with the environment. As we reach him we smile and acknowledge him. He does the same and we get the impression that this is the first time in many days that his leathery face has smiled, how many people have walked passed him today and not spoken. H wonders what state his feet are in if they are encased in wellies all day.

From here we can see the flag of the Omu Refuge but have to drop down, once more, to an exposed col where the rain and wind start to increase, before we get to the final climb. At last we reach the small hut and are not surprised that it was full last year. It is built into the rocks on the summit and appears to be higher than the 'proper' summit that lies a little further on. Also on the top there is what seems to be a weather station together with a large area that looks like it has been the foundations for some older buildings that are long gone. The area is such that you could easily bivouac amongst the debris if needed or even pitch a tent in some places, so we could have risked it last year. We look to the north west towards Bran and think about how last year we intended to take this route through having stayed at Omu, the weather was similar back then but at least the walk out would have been more straight forward than the route we chose.

The way the hut is snuggled in between the rocks means that as we walk around it, we keep discovering doors that have been put in place presumably to allow access to what we assume is a central area which has been boxed in. It really is a bizarre construction that has obviously been built out of necessity for winter conditions up here.

We visit the 'true' summit and try and get some photos of the view before the clouds, once more, close in. Our relative tranquillity on the summit is interrupted with the arrival of a large group of twenty-somethings who dump their rucsacs and immediately crack open some cans of beer to celebrate their ascent. We pick up the track and start the long descent back to the valley. This starts with a series of long zig zags that appear to have been put in place so that pack animals (or possibly quads) can be used to bring up food etc to the hut. My concern for H's knees on a descent like this appear unfounded as she happily launches down the path with no real issues.

On one of the many corners of the path we come across a guardian sheepdog which appears to be in a semi-comatose state, although it does manage to lift its head just long enough to scowl at us before slumping back. Far enough away from the dog we find a nice patch of grass where we sit for lunch. Above we can hear the drunken party from summit as they make their way down, although they appear to go off down a different valley so we are once more left in peace. The dog that we passed earlier on, obviously aware of the food, slowly makes its way towards us but a firm "NO!" from H stops it in its footsteps and it retreats.

Lunch over and we are back to a classic, long, Romanian descent that appears to go on forever. A sign we find gives the vague 6-7 hours for the route down, although we expected it to be a little longer. We pause when we get into the trees to sort gear and hear a rock fall nearby, but what has caused it? We have little doubt it was a bear[125] and

---

[125] This is the area where bears have been descending into the valleys to

there is a large amount of tree damage to confirm their presence. We sing to try and warn them off.

On the opposite hillside clinging on in that way that only they can we spot a pair of chamois picking at the grass and moss that also appears to be defying gravity. We look at the phone app and it shows us that we are on the right side of the stream, despite the fact that it is very poorly marked on the ground and is very overgrown. Whilst the streams are dry at the moment there is thunder and lightning above us and the hills are slowly being engulfed by clouds so it is obviously going to rain up there. Jackets on once more and we brace ourselves for the storm (that never arrives).

We had left the top at around 2pm and had descended for around three hours before we find a water source where we can rest and put a cold compress on H's ankle which has started to swell. The anti-bear singing continues before we finally emerge from the trees onto a track. Here there is a signpost indicating, to the left, a cabana and to the right Busteni. We are, officially, down onto terra firma and whilst there are still a few miles to go at least we are on the flat and working our way through some rather pleasant meadows and trees.

This idyllic walk out of the wilderness soon comes to an abrupt halt as we come across a large wild campsite. It's as if a festival was about to take place and free camping has been offered. There are several hundred tents all the way up the valley and many caravans amongst them. In fact, some of these 'vans look almost permanent judging by the number of

---

scavenge for food out of the dustbins.

exterior features that they have (decking, fencing etc). Although we spot the odd portaloo there appears to be few facilities and the smell drifting over some sections of the site suggest that people are following the bears natural instincts as to where to defecate! The site is not marked on the leaflet that we have but is obviously well known, we even see a party of Scouts emerging from the woods carrying a half pitched tent although it is unclear if it is going up or down. However, what confuses us the most about this site is that, surely, with the amount of abandoned food scattered around that bears must be coming down in an evening to graze?

We join the main track out of the site towards town and soon come across a large entrance arch with a very clear sign saying 'No Camping' in several languages. It also has symbols for no open fires, no cutting down of trees, no picking flowers etc. We get the impression that the area is not well policed!

Beyond the arch and we are in Busteni, exactly where is unclear but we are aware that by just heading downhill we will hit the river, railway and main road. The long route down finally starts to take its toll on H's knees and she is limping quite badly although there are enough properties with strange architectural features to distract her, my personal favourites are those where people have tried to make off road parking by just putting narrow planks over a stream.

Its 7.50pm when we reach the hotel, it has taken us around 6 hours from the summit of Omu. A little like John Mills and Sylvia Syms in Ice Cold In Alex we walk straight into the restaurant dump our rucsacs on the floor (that's not in the film) and order a cold beer – we weren't dressed for the restaurant but we didn't care. It had been a long day. The beers arrives (it's not Carlsberg), is quickly consumed and another is requested.

Food is ordered and H hobbles upstairs to get changed whilst we wait for the food to be cooked, I am content to sit looking like I've just stumbled down from the nearest big hill (which I have!) or washed up on a beach (I'm not wet). H has the trout whilst I, once again, have the Spicy Meat Stew. The food is excellent with the ordering process being made even more entertaining as the waitress speaks little English and we, once more, use the 'two menu method' which involves us trying to match up what the food is by its position in the Romanian menu and the English menu. The waitress is delightful and we even get a smile when H declares success and starts waving a thumbs up at her. With the meal over H decides to order an Ameretto but this is totally lost in translation and she has to go over to the bar and, using what appears to be semaphore, manages to indicate what she is after.

Back at the room we get a phone call from our eldest son who has just been to the funeral of a friend of his who was a regular in the Rook and Gaskell in York where Tom had worked for a period of time. It seems to have shaken him up but strengthened his resolve to move out of London as soon as possible and head back north. He even, once more, talks about taking his driving test[126]. But we think that the main

---

[126] This was the same year as several terrorist incidents in London which, I think, had added to his resolve to get out of the capital.

reason for the call is he just wants a chat with a friendly voice.

Archers listened to and bed.

Thursday 17th August – A Level Results Day. As we are two hours ahead of the UK we watch the whole event unfold on Twitter as different outlets make comments on whether results are up, down or indeed sideways! I have flashbacks to my results coming through. On both occasions I was not at home to receive them and so never experienced the highs (or lows) that are seen on the television. As ever I would guess that the media at home is full of photos of ecstatic, jumping around, pupils whilst giving little thought to those who didn't get what they wanted. Surely there must be a better system? But then I digress. I am in a hotel room in rural Romania – its time for breakfast!

We worked out yesterday, by accident, that the key to breakfast here is to be in and seated before 9am otherwise that is the time that the masses descend. Once more the buffet spread is excellent and we have a quick review of how good the breakfasts have been so far on the trip. The waiter is working his socks off sorting out coffees for everyone and then coming back to the table to check that everything is ok. I order scrambled eggs but end up with a very palatable omelette, I'm not sure how this mix up occurred but am happy with the result.

From our seats we can see that the cloud that was dropping yesterday afternoon has now totally engulfed the mountains We made a good call even though the cloudless morning we had did make it a little warm! Quickly scrap our original plan of going up and over to the next valley on the cable because of the long queue we had yesterday and the cost. Decide instead to have a quieter valley day, this will also give H's knee a chance to recover a little more.

The breakfast discussion now moves onto gin, something I rarely drink and know very little about but H has been reading a book all about it and so is taking this very seriously, but what is the best glass for gin? I put an appeal on Twitter asking that very question and get numerous suggestions (although no definitive one).

In the breakfast area the television is playing modern pop videos on a loop. They all have, roughly, the same plot with gyrating women and dominating men. Many of them then have the men pretending to fire a gun (using their fingers) at the camera. No idea what the songs are about but would guess that the plot of them is similarly as vapid. The adverts in between the videos are predominantly about either food (mainly pizza[127]) or gastric problems (related to pizza?).

We have the usual post-breakfast discussion about what to do next before deciding to walk into Busteni for a mooch around (and to sort the train tickets for tomorrow). As we reach the station first we decide to go and get the tickets before the town.

This is where our plans start to fall apart. The train app we have used throughout our trip (and in 2016) has been

---

[127] We see so many pizza adverts that you really wonder whether it will be the national dish soon.

brilliant and worked out the following for tomorrow morning;

11:22	Busteni
13:10	Bucharest (change)
14:00	Leave Bucharest
16:04	Medgidia (change)
16:22	Medgidia
19:45	Tulcea Oras

This times things perfectly to get us through to the Delta.

We wave the app at the cashier, "No" is her response which is odd as so far she had been very helpful. She spoke little English so I found myself with my head stuck through the hatch staring at her screen as she points at the schedule. It appears that our train does not exist! We fall back to plan B and just get tickets for in the morning that will get us to Bucharest with a view to then sorting it out when we get there although this will leave us a day down. Decision made we buy the tickets and wander back out of the station and into town.

Doubt sets in, "should we have a look at other alternatives?" H says. What we need is some peace and quiet so we can have a good look at how, and when, we can get out to the Delta. Find the perfect place on a bench in the church gardens. The problem appears to be the change at Medgidia (from memory this was an odd place to get to or from but was the main change for going to the Black Sea or the Danube Delta). Our alternatives from here seem far fewer than they were last year but what we do find is a train that leaves Bucharest at 6:40am that would get us into Tulcea for lunchtime with no changes (although it does go through Medgidia). On the back of a serviette I scribble the new plan;

5:33pm	Busteni to Bucharest
6:40am	Bucharest to Tulcea

To proceed with this plan will result in us losing the ticket that we have already paid for and also we will have to do some shuffling around of room bookings. However, it does mean that in 24 hours time we will be in Tulcea on the banks of the Danube so the decision is made. We are heading East.

We book a room at the Ibis in Bucharest for tonight (cheap and cheerful) and head back to the ticket office.
Unsurprisingly she remembers us! Yes, we can cancel but there is a 10% cancellation/charge, but we can't book on the 5:33pm train as it "has already left" (very kindly translated by a gentleman behind us).
What about the 6:13pm? That will do nicely. I mention about tickets to the Delta and she sorts us out with those tickets as well. So we have tickets to Bucharest, a room booked in Bucharest and then tickets for onward transmission to Tulcea.

Last year we referred to our trip out to Tulcea as our 'Dash to the Delta' even though it was a calm, orderly trip. Now we have to dash back to the hotel, explain what is happening, pack and then dash back to the station before we even start with our trip out to the Delta.

The owner is not on the desk when we get back to the hotel but, fortunately, the receptionist understands what is happening (and doesn't really bat an eyelid). We point out to her that we will still pay for the room as it is our fault that we have messed them about and, as the hotel is busy, they may have missed out on a booking. Back at the room we just make sure that everything is wedged in the rucsacs, everything can be repacked in Bucharest – let's just get going.

Then it's off back to the station.

We realise that we have had nothing to eat since breakfast and probably won't get anything this evening in Bucharest, so, with an hour to go before the train departs, we find ourselves in an odd Romanian restaurant with lots of animal pelts on the wall, waiting for food. H keeps looking at her watch as if that will make a difference. Whatever happens it's going to be a close run thing to eat, pay and get on the train and H's 'They always run late" mantra may not be the best part of the plan (although probably the only one we can guarantee).

The food arrives on a tray with both courses wedged on (soup and main) and we realise that this is very much a churn them through type of restaurant rather than one that concentrates on the eating experience. The soup gets a thumbs up from both of us and the gravy that comes with my pork has the consistency of a stew. Sadly the chips are a little mass produced but considering the whole lot came in for under ten pounds (including a couple of Ciuc Radlers) then we can't complain. All sorted and to the station with twenty minutes to spare. Even had time to get some bread for tomorrow's journey (1 RON) from a bakery that appeared to be someone's kitchen.

The signs on the platform are more confusing than usual as we discover that the original train we were going for has been delayed and is now behind us! We are looking for wagon 1A which, logic suggests, is behind or at least near wagon 1. But when the train arrives the number are all over the place; 23, then 22, 21, 20 then 1! We get on board and make our way through guessing that ours is 'along here somewhere!'. Initially, this also involves hitting lots of people with our hipbelts until we fasten them back. H asks "Is this 1B?" of a helpful looking woman, "No, this is 1". This means that there are two number 1s - we are well and truly confused! Make our way into the next carriage under the impression that it is 1, 1A, 1B. Wrong again, we come across 25 and 26, then first class. We decide to take the only logical course of action and stay put until the guard arrives. The train will only make three stops before Bucharest and ten minutes after leaving we get to Sinai.

The guard arrives and tells us that we are not in 1B, this is carriage 2 (I hope that you are keeping up with this at the back). Rather confused I point towards the second carriage, where we had been told we were in carriage 1, the guard agrees. We start to get up but, maybe realising that this may cause more hassle down the carriage, she gestures to us to sit down and say, nicely, "stay here!". So we do!

Its only 20 degrees outside so its reassuring that the air conditioning is working overtime, we hope that the train to the Delta tomorrow has a similar system in place (but are pretty sure that it will not!). As we head south we have the views of Romania that we have got used to with bee wagons, unfinished buildings, abandoned factories and rivers that have had attempts made to harness their power (normally unsuccessfully). A beggar approaches me and makes an appeal in Romanian, I shrug my shoulders and say "I'm English". She tuts and wanders off down the carriage to annoy someone else.

The train journey passes very smoothly[128], the carriages are clean, the toilets well washed and so on. It seems very odd.

Arrive in Bucharest five minutes late (of course) and are immediately thrown back into the hustle, bustle and general noisiness of a big city. After a few weeks traveling around 'the provinces' it is something of a culture shock. We know our way to the Ibis, its walking distance, and so don't need a taxi but still expect to be approached by the multiple taxi drivers outside the station. It doesn't happen, which is strange, although after H's tirade at them last year maybe she is listed as being someone to avoid.

It's easy to find our way to the Ibis; left out of the station, past the sex shop on the corner, then right at the next junction where the security guard at the building site was wearing what appeared to be caving knee pads.

We book in, quickly getting the Newby Cat pleasantries out of the way and then come the excuses from the hotel.

"I am sorry but we do not have a double room, only a twin"
"That's ok, we'll manage"
"....and also I only have a smoking room so you may have to open the window!"

---

[128] Not an expression that I use very often when referring to Romanian trains.

"It's only for one night"

"Also, the bed is in kit form and you will have to make it up!", ok so I made that bit up, although we were expecting it. Then it's the usual route up to what seems like the three hundredth floor, such is the length of time we spend in the lift, with people getting on and off at various points on the way.

We walk in and H sums up the condition of the room, "Someone has died in here!". It does have an odd smell, but as we said, "its only for one night" and there is no sign of a dead body. We wrestle with the air conditioning and television, eventually get them both functioning with a minimum amount of kicking. A similar effort has to be made to open the window but we just hide the ashtrays in a drawer to reduce the smell. The room is definitely in need of refurbishment.

There are two beds, a queen size and a single (which we use for storage).

After a little discussion we decide that going to the bar for a beer is not a good idea as we have an early start tomorrow. In preparation for this we pack the rucsacs as well as we can and shower. Say what you like about the Ibis but the showers are wonderful.

Friday 18th August – Reasonable, if a little restless, nights sleep. The air conditioning, as we expect in the Ibis, makes a gentle chugging sound all night as it strains to keep going. Evidence of its previous efforts are clear from the number of broken panels on the top of the unit. Still it keeps the cheese, that is carefully stored in the bottom of wardrobe, reasonably cool.

Last night we hatched a cunning plan to make sure that we are up in time with both phones set for slightly staggered times. We also have the curtains open and our watch alarms on.

Wake up at midnight convinced that its time to get up before falling asleep listening to the More or Less Podcast. Nothing better than statistics to put you to sleep.

5:15   The first alarm goes off on my side so is easily turned off. H sleeps on.
5:20   H's phone goes off, which is on the other side of the room. She stirs saying   "Waz a eem is….?" which I take to mean "What time is it?" and so tell her   its 5:30 (the agreed get up time). She rolls over and goes back to sleep   whilst I get up.
5.30   (Real time), H opens her eyes and in one(ish) move gets up. A lot of   stumbling is involved but at least she is moving.

Put the news on, it leads with details about a van attack in Barcelona.

Our alarms keep going off for the next thirty minutes before we cancel them.

We leave the room at 6am and eventually find ourselves in reception (the hotel appears to have some sort of lock down in the night to stop people wandering around so we struggle to find the exit off our floor). We check out, hand in the key card, and head out into a pleasantly cool Bucharest morning retracing our route, past the security guard (the replacement has no knee pads), the sex shop and the taxi rank. Having already got our tickets we don't have to join the long queues at the ticket office.

Coffee is called for and H gets some from the little kiosk that has opened in the station, it resembles a rather large egg with the assistant slotted in somehow (I do a couple of laps to work out where the door to it is but fail). We also get a couple of sausage rolls, for breakfast, and head for Platform 13. The platform is easy to find but somewhere to sit is not as most of the chairs on the platform have been broken. Improvisation is called for and we just sit on our rucsacs whilst we wait for the train to arrive.

The train arrives on time and, to our surprise, it's a nice modern one. We conclude that this is the case as it's the through train to the Delta[129]. On we get and easily find our seats. Opposite are a Romanian couple whose luggage appears to be several large bags of food and a laptop bag. By comparison, with our large rucsacs, we appear to be over equipped. Our view of the outside world from the train is somewhat blocked by some graffiti on the outside of the train, on the plus side it goes give us some extra shade.

6:41 and we leave. As soon as the train starts to move the woman opposite us gets up and starts to wander down the train, muttering something to her partner. The guard arrives soon after to check tickets at which point the man

---

[129] Last year we had to change to a rather rough train that appeared to have been put together from scrap parts.

gets up, says something and wanders off down the train, are they fair dodgers or just looking for better seats. As I look up and down the train I notice that many of our fellow passengers are starting to snuggle down ready for the five hour journey with blankets and pillows extracted from their travel bags.

Whilst we are getting our Kindles cranked up the wandering couple return, retrieve their gear a little at a time and ferry it to wherever they have found new seats. Their places are taken by two Mario Bros lookalikes who just sit and stare out of the window, or at least stare at the graffiti beyond which I'm sure there are views.

We appear to stop at every station before Medgidia although at some it only appears to be a pause, for the driver to wave at the stationmaster perhaps? Finally we reach Medgidia where almost the entire train empties onto the platform for a cigarette (and some dash into the nearby bar for a quick beer). Five minutes later, everyone is back on board and we head north through mile after of mile of agricultural land. A new addition (at least since last year) is the number of wind turbines that have appeared in this area and all the way up to Tulcea. This time there are deliberate stops at the stations on the way and we lose people at various towns/villages and in some places just buildings!

Arrive at Tulcea only a few minutes late. Considering the time we have travelled it's practically on time! As the usual bun fight takes place we wait and are the last off the train and onto the platform. Most of the other passengers are running to the station building and going through it at speed Having been here before we know that the short cut is around the outside and onto the promenade. At the far end of which is the Hotel Delta.

In the heat of the midday sun we make our way along trying to pick out any pieces of shade we can. After doing this for a few minutes we conclude that the direct, unshaded, route it probably the best and make a beeline for the hotel. On the way here we had spoken of trying to find a boat for hire to take us into the Delta but most appear to be out, or not really sea worthy, so the air conditioned hotel offers us an excellent oasis.

"Hello, we have a reservation.......we are Newby Cat", we wait for the usual reply but instead get.
"Oh yes, we are expecting you. You have stayed with us before", and there it was, acknowledgement of our previous visit. It was a statement, not a question. We feel special.
"Er yes, this time last year", to which they even give us the date.

We have no need to hand over our passports as we are already on the system and our details are printed off for us to sign.

"Your room is not yet ready. The cleaner is.....er.....what is the word?"
"Cleaning?" we say in unison
"No....she's er......"
Both of the receptionist start miming a hoovering action.
"Hoovering?"
They both look puzzled.
"Vacuuming?"
"Da!"

Initially we try and explain the difference in the two but give up.

"We'll go and have a drink", and retire to the large inside bar area for a lemonade (for H) and a, rather disappointing, frappe for me. Outside the intensity of the sun has forced many people under the canopies and umbrellas which adorn the terraced area and there are few signs of mad dogs, or Englishmen out there.

Our key card is brought to us and the receptionist apologies for the delay, in the spirit of friendliness, we apologies for being early!

Room 228, we go in and find that, yes, we do have a balcony and a view over the Danube towards Ukraine. Rucsacs, which have not really been properly sorted since Brasov, are rather unceremoniously emptied onto the floor, then shuffled into the drawers before we both fall asleep for a couple of hours (the fitful night's sleep and early start catching up with us).

Catch the original Cocoon, with Steve Guttenberg, as we tidy up before heading out to find a Tourist Information Office (there are two marked on the map). We hope to try and find out about getting out to the Black Sea at Sfantu Gheirghe and also about day trips into the Delta. Of course we don't hold out much hope but it will give us a starting point.

Its still very hot outside as we reach the Office only to find that it is closed, a helpful sign informs us that it closes at 4pm on a Friday and doesn't open on a Saturday or Sunday. A second sign informs us where the other office is, but of course, we find that it is also closed (and doesn't open on

Saturday or Sunday either). The detour to the second office has left us away from the river and so we make our way through some very strange areas of town (via a shop for water) back to the Promenade in search of a boat that will take us into the Delta tomorrow. Yes, there are places on some of the larger vessels but we fancy something smaller that will take us deeper in but very few of these are available. Eventually we come across a very odd looking bloke who speaks no English (although good Spanish and Italian), he has a boat that will float in very little water (he describes this through mime) and will take us out for three hours for 200RON. We just need to be at Laura (his main boat), near the train station for 9am.

We shake on it and set off to find Laura which is near the 'white building', I pick up on the 'bianco' bit. He also points out a red car as a further navigational aid. I find the boat with no problems (H has given up the hunt and sat down). Our captain (?) has got there first on his bike and he invites me on board but I, politely, decline. Reassuringly he waves the life jackets at me just to prove he has them!

Catch up with H and back to the room for a hotel picnic overlooking the Danube. Clothes washed and sorted.

The news announces that Bruce Forsyth has passed away.

Saturday 18th August – Think it was a good night's sleep, although it took a few attempts to get through one of the podcasts on Korea. The hotel is very quiet and a total contrast to Busteni, even with the doors to the balcony open the only real noise you can hear is the odd blast on a ship's whistle as we are, effectively, at the end of the road (and the road to the hotel is at the other side of the building). Even the Ibis had the gentle chugging of the air conditioning unit.

We are fully awake just after 6.30 (even H) and down to the restaurant for 7 for breakfast. Its relatively busy with people obviously getting fed before heading off into the Delta. The buffet spread is as substantial as we remember and has the best selection of cold meats and cheeses that we have come across so far, not to mention the fact there are puddings as well. As we eat a serviette is brought into service to plan the rest of the trip;

Sunday - Sfantu Gheorghe (St George) and camp there for two nights.
Tuesday – back to Tulcea then to Constanta, via Medgidia, and stay there for three nights.
Friday – Bucharest for hotel overnight before AirBnB.

This assumes several things; mainly that we can get to St G (we know there is a ferry but beyond that nothing) and does the train to Constanta exists, as my faith in the Train App has been knocked.

But first we turn our attention to finding the boat Laura and our captain for today. It's a lovely cool morning as we head along the promenade and whilst many of the shops are still closed the bars are doing a roaring trade for breakfast. We are at the station in double quick time and as we look round 'John', as we discover he is called, arrives on his bike with provisions and greets us with a rather jolly "Good morning sir" before beckoning us on board Laura. The small boat that we are going to be touring the Delta on is tied up at the other side with a narrow plank having to be negotiated to get on board (for plank read two pieces of pallet wood that have been nailed together).

On board, if that's what it can be called, we are issued with life jackets and even John wears one. The boat is a cross between an open canoe and the traditional Lipovan fishing vessel obviously designed specifically for this sort of journey. John cranks up the motor (it takes a couple of attempts and even then sounds like a forty a day smoker until it settles down) and off we go. We have specifically chosen this type of vessel as it will go in shallow water away from the larger vessels that are currently buzzing around us creating rather substantial swells. Any thoughts that I have about the boat being unstable are quickly forgotten as we comfortably cut through the waves before turning off the main waterways and into some very narrow channels, away from the masses and peace appears to descend. We move forward very slowly and find ourselves on the edge of a lagoon with large groups of pelicans, various types of stork, cormorants and even a turtle. We both comment about the number of photographs that we are taking compared to how many we would have taken had it been in the pre-digital age.

The quiet tour is over all too soon as we have to head back to the main channel and join the lanes with the larger cruise style ships. Some of these appear to be moored up having lunch, not sure if this is before or after they head into the Delta. We cross the main river channel in order to 'drive on the left', pass the old catamaran which has been dry docked for some time and then past a few, well painted, Romanian Navy vessels (last year they were all out in the Black Sea for an exercise).

We dock, hand back our life jackets and pay him. John immediately turns to the occupant of the next boat and says something in Romanian that I assume is "When they've gone do you want to go to the pub?" H takes the obligatory selfie before we shake hands and head back to the hotel.

The sun is well up as we head back and we are happy to get into a nearby bar for a Radler and a lemonade. Our long sleeved shirts (essential for the Delta trip) are removed, H pushes her's into her bag whilst I hang mine on the back of a chair to dry. We pay and head to the small kiosks for a doughy thing and to find a wide brimmed hat for H, for the trip down to St G. Doughy thing purchased but no success with the hat, it appears that you can only really get captain's hats. On the plus side we find where, we think, the ferry to St G goes from. All we need to do now is work out where to get tickets!

As we leave the jetty I realise that I have left my long sleeved shirt on the back of the chair at the bar we stopped in and head back to collect it, of course someone has handed it in and it is safely stowed behind reception (I apologise for its sweatiness!). Reunited we head back for some air conditioning as the town appears to take something of a siesta. On the TV is the start of Maid in Manhattan so we decide to head down to the swimming pool instead. First it's a few lengths until it starts to fill up with people who are doing widths (they obviously watched the film a little longer than us) and then it's into the, very, warm bubbly pool. On the way out we notice that there is a large JPS[130] watch by the door which looks about as conspicuous as you could get.

---

[130] John Player Special were a cigarette company who sponsored the

Head back to the room and catch the end of Maid in Manhattan, I am pretty sure that we saw the best bits and invested the time in the middle more wisely. A bit of internet searching reveals where we need to purchase tickets from and confirms the times for the ferry tomorrow. The good news is that it is a later start than we expected and so we are in no rush. This means that we can get fresh provisions sorted before we head off.

Dinner is another Danube Delta Hotel Picnic as we finish off all of the food that we have before stocking up in the morning. H finds the last of the wine and we also managed to boil some water for a cup of tea.

It's the end of a busy day and, whilst we still have no idea where to get the tickets for the ferry to St G from we are confident that we can head towards the Black Sea tomorrow. H sits on the balcony until the sun sets, and the mosquitoes arrive, then scuttles back inside. We discover that the locking mechanism on the door is broken and so wedge the door shut with a table and make a note to tell reception when we leave.

Sunday 20th August – three weeks ago we were at a wedding back in Rotherham and now we are on the banks of the Danube listening to a profile of Taylor Swift on Radio 4 (probably the only time we'll hear her on the station). Head down for breakfast, no rush this morning as the ferry is not until noon. What we do realise is that its going to be a long

---

Lotus team in the 1970s. Their black and gold livery was very distinctive. It would appear that this watch is a throwback to the big advertising campaigns that took place.

time before our next breakfast of this nature and so stock up on lots of meat, cheese, eggs and more meat. For the first time this trip I go for the melon having been put off by the over consumption of it last year when we stayed in Brasov[13]

The breakfast area is surprisingly quiet and we conclude that our late start, 8am, has caused us to miss the early, heading for the boat trips, rush. As we get up to leave at around 9.30 we realise that this is not the case as everyone starts arriving! Back to the room and pack the rucsacs for the journey. Fortunately the booking out time is noon so we can leave them there whilst we have one last wander around Tulcea. Head for the aquarium that had so impressed us last year not expecting it to open until 10 but it is, 30 RON well spent and we immediately head for the basement where all the sturgeon etc are in their tanks. Lots of great information about the Delta and its flora and fauna. We now split up as H heads back to the room for a shower whilst I go to the supermarket to get food for the journey (bread, cheese, sausage etc). As I queue up at the til to pay the man in front of me declares that he has no money. Is this a scam whereby he gets other people to offer to pay for him? I wonder whether I should pay, it's only a few RON. But is it a scam,? I so it's not a very big one! As I hesitate he finds some money in his jacket and pays.

Head back to the Hotel walking past one of the 24 hour gambling outlets where someone is just leaving. As they do they pause outside and hand a bundle of notes to a girl by the door before carrying on their way. There is no exchange of words. I walk passed to avoid getting dragged in.

---

[131] See the first book.

As H finishes the last of her sorting I try once more to fix the door, but without success. On the plus side I do work out exactly what the problem is, it needs a new locking mechanism as a piece of it has broken off.

Go to book out realising that we now have no accommodation arranged for the next week (basically until Bucharest). The sort of plan we like. At reception we are asked if we have enjoyed our stay;

"Yes, thank you, very enjoyable"
"Good, you will come again, yes?"
"Next time we are in the area we will. By the way we must mention that the door for the balcony is broken"
"What is wrong?"
"It won't close properly and the lock doesn't work"
"OK"
She seems both quite interested but at the same time not really bothered, a wonderful juxtaposition that some Romanian hotel staff can do so wonderfully.

We walk out onto the promenade and head towards the terminal to buy tickets, but where and how? One website says that the ferry runs on a Sunday but another one says that it does not. The Tourist Information says that it does but the hotel says not. We find a seat near what we think is the office and surf the Internet to see what we can find but without success. H in the end concludes that attack is the best form of defence and I am despatched to get tickets from the station (although most of the references that we find say you cannot buy them until an hour before). I join the small queue that has formed.

"Good morning, two tickets for St George?" I make it more of an inquisitive question than a request, hoping that will help.
"OK", says the cashier smiling back at me, "96 lei"
I hand over the money and she hands me the tickets.
"Platform Three" and gestures down the promenade. Sorted good customer service with simple language.
Much simpler than I thought.

About 12.15 we walk down to the berth and get on board.
On the way H sees, and buys, a hat for the journey.[132]

On board H, of course, immediately falls into conversation with a Romanian family. He works for a bank and their daughter has just been to English Camp so they tease her to talk to us! H plays up to the teasing. After a few minutes we decide that where we are is going to be too hot and so move to the front of the boat where there is a nice sea breeze. Our new friends follow us as we spread our gear out to make if more comfortable, our rucsacs once more being used as seats.

The family are from Bucharest and are staying at St G until 1st September, which judging from what we have read about what there is to do seems like a long time. John works in banking and deals with cross-border monetary exchanges. We chat briefly about leasing equipment after I make reference to my old role in the bank and establish a bond. Together with their son and daughter they have a two year old dog called Mia who is very nervous about being on a boat but settles down now we have moved to the front.

---

[132] Usual last minute planning.

Four and a half hours. Do you know how long that is, bobbing up and down in a large biscuit tin? Here's a clue, it's a very long time! Apart from sitting on the rucsacs we have no real seating and spend much of the journey standing chatting to John and his family. He pulls out a couple of cans of what he refers to as "nice" Romanian beer (7+%), one for him and one for me, then turns and apologises to H for not having more. When John finds out that we have done this sort of trip before H points out that I have written a book about it and suggests he buys it.

Conversation continues in fits and starts as the journey progresses with the rest of the time either taking photographs or reading. On both sides there is little to see but trees[133].

A couple of boys come up to the front and start messing with the ship's bell, which until this point, had been left alone. H tells them off and the bell ringing stops, although one of them keeps looking at her wondering whether he can push the boundaries a little more. In the end he doesn't risk it as ending up in the Danube may have offended.

Finally we dock, say farewell to John and family (exchange contact details as he wants to make sure that we are ok this evening) and set off down a long track to the Green Dolphin to camp[134].

---

[133] We are reminded of a long train journey we took in Scandinavia in the late 1980s where all we could see were trees for hour after hour.
[134] We later discover that its two kilometres which, in the heat of the day, is quite a way.

Camp Reception and we find that the assistant speaks excellent English. We comment about not seeing any English people and how we are happy with that. A couple of Germans behind us agree and we all laugh. We are given a price to camp and as we are about to complete the paperwork H asks after the beach huts that are for rent, at £40 for two nights it's a no brainer and we find ourselves in a rather pleasant garden shed with two beds, a light and an electrical socket. The site appears to be an upgrade of the site we stayed at in Turda last year. Dump our rucsacs and head straight to the bar area for food.

Beer purchased from a rather grandiose bar area and then we try and work out how to order food. We ask the bar tender who waves us over to the far end of the seating area and we go to a little hut. Here we work out what we want and pay for it, simple so far. Now Romanian bureaucracy and complexity kicks in. We are given a receipt that we take to a larger hut, that contains the kitchen area (such as it is), hand it over and our food is prepared. We have the *Evening Special* which is polenta, cottage cheese and sausage with a side order of mixed pickles. Sadly it's served on plastic plates which we feel spoils their eco-friendly attitude. I am sent back to the bar so H can have her second Hugo, although my accent means that I take three attempts (and a lot of pointing at the sign) before she understands me. We finish off the food with a Betty Ice choc bar, exactly what is needed here where the temperature appears to have changed little from when we got off the boat several hours ago and it is still in the high thirties.

Retire to our hut. Inside it is very hot but if we open the door then the mosquitoes will just fly in and get us. H comes up with a solution and we pin up her sarong across the door and wedge a rucsac underneath it to fill in the gap. Its not ideal but it works well enough. Outside, near the bar, is a large outdoor cinema screen and around 9pm a film starts, after a bit of effort we work out that it's A Beautiful Mind. We discuss the possibility of going to watch it but decide that the mosquitoes would make it too uncomfortable, crank up the iPods and snuggle down.

Week Four

Monday 21ˢᵗ August – We are, probably, at the further east of the trip so our task from here is to make our way to the Black Sea, which is about two kilometres along the track heading east, to draw a line in the sand indicating that we can go no further.

Last night, despite the film playing away in the background we fell asleep quite easily. Initially it was rather a sweaty slumber until around midnight when the temperature became more tolerable. H even had her woollen blanket on[1]

8am and I wake up. Technically that constitutes a lie in compared to what we have been used to over recent days. So what to do for breakfast and what to do today? The research that we have done on the area, such as it is, suggests that St G is not quite a full throttle destination so we decide to spend the morning exploring the town and then the beach this afternoon. But first we try and find some morning coffee. The on site café is closed so its from a machine! Oddly the brown goo is really nice and drinkable, which really surprises us as the machine ones usually appear to contain a large amount of grit to bulk it out! In this *Bohemian Paradise* we expected some weird flavoured things so something as normal as the coffee comes as a pleasant surprise. By the time we realise that we can get breakfast from the café, as it is about to open, we have already consumed the last of our travelling bread and the

---

[135] The hut comes with twin beds/benches with sheets and a blanket that is one up from a traditional army blanket. We choose to use our silk sleeping bag liners.

cheese that is left. Sadly the large tomato didn't make it and is given as rather ignominious burial as it is dumped in the bin.

The dogs on the site (we have only seen one cat) are all spread out on the floor in little sand hollows trying to rest after last night's barking with some of the ground staff finding amusement from brushing the sand onto them. The dogs hardly move and don't even manage to raise a scowl at the staff.

Change of hat for H (the other, new one, was too wind sensitive) and we walk into St G. One of the main reasons for this (the beach is in the opposite direction) is to find out where we catch the ferry from in the morning, where we pay and so on (it's always good to try and sort your escape route out before anything else).

St G seems like a lovely place but maybe that opinion is influenced by it being so hot and there's not a lot to it! There's a church, a bank, a supermarket and (signs for) a couple of restaurants all within 10 minutes' walk of each other. But that appears to be it. I think that people come here to get away from it all and for that it's excellent as there are very few distractions of any kind.

We find a sign pointing to the docks and follow it before we pick up a sign for the ticket office. As ever with these signs we are taken on a rather circuitous route before the signs just run out. We make our way up to the dock where we find a sign that suggests that the ticket office is behind a small door to the right. There is no sign on the door but it is the only possible place where it could be hiding. We decide that a visit later in the evening may be a good idea. We head back into town.

Having earlier seen a Land Rover (and trailer) that appeared to be acting as transport out to the beach we make our way back onto the main strip, passed a building site where a lot of standing around is being done before we reach a bench that appears to be a stopping point for the beach transport. An 'air conditioned' minibus pulls up – 3RON to the beach and we get on-board. As we expect not only is the air conditioning working away but the driver has all of the windows open, as well as the sliding door fully open. We don't try and tell him that this is not a good idea as we zoom off along the dirt track. He is too busy talking on his mobile to engage in conversation anyway and too busy to stow the fare that we have paid him carefully, it is just thrown into a space in front of the speedometer. The track goes past the campsite before suddenly the ground changes into beach which makes no difference to our speed as our driver keeps his foot down until we come to a, sort of, turning circle (or a sand trap!) where we grind to a halt.

Romania is not very big on warning signs. To be honest they are not very big on useful signs in many places as our hunt for the booking office this morning proved. So when we see a huge sign warning us of the danger of swimming in the Danube Channel (where is meets the Black Sea) then we conclude that this is quite important and make a mental note
  The only other sign says "The Beach" and so, as a safer

---

[136] In fact it is nearly impossible to get to the edge of the Danube Channel from where we were unless you were very determined, not afraid of getting cut to pieces by the undergrowth or worried about being attacked by sand snakes!

option, we go that way and come across a bar. The sun is up so its time for a Radler to cool off. This cheers up the bar staff who impress us with their unique way of removing the bottle tops by, effectively, hitting it with the bottle opener sending the top flying off in a random direction. One of the staff offers to teach me how to do it but I point out that I am more old school and hitting it on the side of a wall is more my style[137].

The bar is a temporary 'popup' one, presumably here for the season and the staff accommodation appears to be the provided by several caravans that are tucked away in the sand dunes with the portaloos. Beneath the bar there is a glass display cabinet with lots of souvenirs for sale that fall somewhere between Blackpool *Kiss Me Quick* hats and plastic garden gnomes! We resist the temptation to buy a "I've seen the Black Sea" pebble"[138]

The seating is either basic, back breaking scatter cushion type bean bags or good practical, sink in the sand, plastic chairs. We go for the plastic ones. Opposite us sit a Romanian couple who are looking at air flights on their phones (of course there is free Wifi here) and we hear both WizzAir and EasyJet mentioned. This prompts us to wonder if there is an airport closer than the one at Bucharest. A sign near the bar says "Friends Gather Here" with a couple of pelicans on it and it does seem to be a gathering place for all. On the other side of the track is a further seated area that is under a large piece of tarpaulin and, looking at the people

---

[137] This is a lie as (1) it lacks style and (2) it usually results in a broken bottle.
[138] Does exactly what it says. It was just a pebble (possibly from the Black Sea area) with a message painted on it, maybe with Tippex?

under it, appears to be much warmer than where we are. As the Romanian couple get up to leave we are treated to a display of bottle juggling as the girls restock the beer fridges by throwing the bottle to each other – I suppose that you have to do something to pass the time.

H wanders off to check out the toilets and get changed.

A few Germans walk up to the bar and immediately start talking English to the staff rather than trying German. One o them smiles at me and says "Good Morning" in near perfect English. As it's getting close to the hottest part of the day we decide to wait in the shade a little longer and order a coffee. This wait is made even longer as we are forgotten about and when H goes to ask after them she finds the cups sitting on the side of the bar. Concluding that the cloud that is gathering is not going to shield us from the sun we set off along the track to the beach almost immediately coming across another warning sign saying "Do Not Swim In The Bit Where The Danube Meets The Black Sea Or You Will Die"[139]. This is to the right so we follow everyone else to the left onto a vast stretch of beach that goes on as far as the eye can see.

As we walk along the hot sand we meet John and his family, complete with Mia who appears to have been in the water. We pause briefly to talk to them and John informs us that she has been in the water but not for very long and is still a little nervous, although she seems fine to us. The kids are sitting on a large inflatable sofa that they have brought, reading. We tell them that we are planning to have a walk

---

[139] I paraphrase

down the beach before going for a swim. John holds up his book and points out that he has a lot of reading to do!

It is not long before we lose the crowds and almost have the beach to ourselves. I say almost as there is a naked middle aged couple who are casually wandering down the beach away from the crowds and a heavily tattooed man (also naked) who is meditating in an area that he has cordoned off with stones for peace and quiet. What is clear is that there is plenty of beach to go around as it disappears into the distance towards Sulina (Romania's most easterly point).

We have a brief explore inland from the beach in the hope of finding some wildlife. Of course it's too hot and all we see are lots of gulls and cormorants. A runner (in this heat?) appears from the busy area and disappears to the north looking like the reverse of the character who appears from the desert to Lawrence of Arabia. Having failed to find anything of interest (there is a decaying building slightly inland of us but that's it) we head back to the main section of beach and continue north towards a herd of cows that have wandered onto the beach. Beyond the cattle there is a small blue (Decathlon?) pop up tent which we have been using as a marker to head towards. Beyond that there is just more and more beach.

We pause for lunch which is an apple and a Fagaras bar.

H decides that we have walked far enough and when we look back, and can't see anyone (or any thing), I have to conclude that she is right. We start to head back and decide that a paddle in the Black Sea is in order and whilst it is a bit *silty* it is warm. A paddle leads to a full blown swim. I think about the warning signs as we entered the area but we must be at least two miles from the inlet and the only vessels we can see are so far away I would think that they are in Ukraine waters. H gets a little spooked when some shrimp type animals skit across her feet as she goes in. A great place for a dip, far enough away from the crowds to have some peace and quiet but close enough for death not to be an issue if anything happens. We dry off and wander back towards civilisation (such as it is). On the way we see a couple who are performing some aquatic gymnastics where he is projecting her into the air so she can perform a near perfect backwards somersault, both are of course naked. The naked meditator doesn't seem to have moved at all in the almost three hours that we have been out.

John and family are also where we left them earlier. We try and explain where we have been but John, lacking his glasses, is struggling to see anything beyond a few metres. We gesture up the coast and say "a long way!". They are staying another hour before heading back into town so we say bye (again) and head off. Mia is obviously overcoming her fear of water as she is soaking wet.

We have just missed the transport back to the town so we head back to the, still busy, bar.

"Two Radlers please"
"Bottle or can?", comes the reply from the bottle top flipping bar staff.
"Which is cold?"
"They are both cold"
"Which do you have most of?", this is my stock reply when I am struggling to decide what to buy.

She hesitates.

"You want us to have bottles so you can do your little trick"

She smiles, pulls two bottles out of the fridge and the tops are quickly despatched. The people behind us are impressed and there is a little round of applause.

"You love doing that, don't you?"

She laughs.

I turn to the crowd, "She's available for parties if you ask nicely", that gives us a few more laughs.

Sitting, drinking our Radlers, we ponder on when the bar closes. Its now 5pm and starting to get quiet but the beach is still very busy and I'm sure that there is business to be had from them. Radlers finished we thank the cabaret act (ie the bar staff) and wait for the transport back to town. As ever it's a case of playing Romanian Transport Roulette and end up getting into what appears to be an airport baggage trailer being towed behind an old Land Rover. Sitting in the trailer we note the lack of any real coupling device between us and the Land Rover. This results in the hitch keeping grounding whenever we go over the slightest bump (of which there are many).

The journey is as interesting as it is dangerous as some people are hanging onto the outside of the trailer (it is worth pointing out that they still have to pay full fare for the adventure).

A little shaken we arrive in town and set out to find the very well advertised pizza restaurant. Neither of us really fancies pizza but places to eat are somewhat limited. We follow the signs and sit down in the restaurant (loose description as it resembles someone's front garden). Sadly there appears to be no system in place where you order food (or for that matter, pay for food). The locals appear to be wandering in and out of the various buildings but no one is bringing out food. It looks like another, over complicated, 'order there…..pay there…..pick up there!' system that no one understands. H goes to investigate and returns with beer. I have a Romanian Ciuc whilst H has a New Zealand Old Moot (still struggling to find a local cider). As we look around a small window opens in one of the numerous buildings, does this mean that the kitchens are, maybe, open?

A German couple arrive and ask us how you order, we throw up our arms and say we have no idea but believe you may have to order "…from that window…", like us they decide that a drink is in order before they work out the food system Judging from their heavy duty rucsacs and other gear we conclude that they are cavers or serious water sports enthusiasts.

We look at our current position, we have travelled over nine hours to get here (5+ from Bucharest to Tulcea then 4+ from Tulcea to St G). Curiosity gets the better of us as we work out that it would take us 9 hours and 20 minutes to drive from home to Durness Beach in North Scotland. An interesting comparison.

Time passes and, together with the Germans, we abandon the idea of ordering food from here and head to the supermarket that we had spotted earlier. As with many of these types of shops there are no windows and the interior goes on much further than first appears. It is well stocked with four staff replenishing the shelves as people returning from the beach buy food (rather than get confused by the pizza restaurant?). What the manager does not appear to have done is manage the logistics very well as they only have one person on the tills. This results in a very long queue. Thirty minutes later and this is noticed. One of the stackers is drafted in to help, but only selling cigarettes (which are behind the counter). This has the desired result and the queue all but disappears.

Make our way back up to the ferry terminal where the "fast ferry" for tomorrow is docked and being replenished for the return trip. Fortune smiles on us and the booking "office" is open. To call it an office is making it wonderfully grandiose, a cupboard would be more accurate and a small cupboard at that! On the security side it is at least behind a large, bombproof door. The desk is manned by a bored looking woman whose eyes light up when she sees two odd looking English people walking up to her. Even with no language compatibility we purchase tickets easily. This is mainly achieved by waving at the boat next to us and saying "Tulcea". It will mean an early start so that we can get the linking train from there to head south.

On the way back to the campsite we decide to have a look at what is on offer at the complex across the track from us which consists of a group of high specification holiday lodges, hotel and (more importantly) a restaurant. Some of the items on the menu look quite inviting and we decide to ask after table availability. At this point we are approached by a rather slimey waiter, who has been observing our movements in the same way as some museum staff do[140]. He informs us that they are not doing anything on the menu this

---

[140] As if we are about to steal everything!

evening as "Today we are having a Turkish evening......it is twenty Euro per person". We look him up and down in the same way as he has eyed us and decide that we will go and eat the meal of the day across at the site. H notices that the restaurant is about a quarter full so it looks as if either no one fancied the Turkish cuisine, or the waiter was too smug to everyone and put them off.

Back in the comfort and far more pleasant surroundings of the campsite's food area we ask what the food is today, "Pork mush, sausages and polenta". We order two and take part in the, now well choreographed, food purchasing dance. When it arrives we find that the pork mush is a type of stew with some spicy sausages thrown in for good measure. Once more the Romanians managed to make something very palatable out of odds and ends. Polenta skulks at the side of the place absorbing the juice from the stew just to add to the meal. A couple of bottles of Ciuc later and we head back to the hut to pack ready for an early start tomorrow.

Tonight's film is Clint Eastwood's Million Dollar Baby which gives us the added disturbance of being surprised every time a bell rings (and the sound of it then echoing around the site and the dogs barking). Remembering that it's a boxing film this means that it is happening a lot!

As it's a stiller evening we are more aware of the mosquitoes than we were last night, do a couple of sweeps and some sarong readjustments to get them out. As we start to bed down H sits up with a start as a beetle buzzes passed her. Despite our best efforts we fail to find it and snuggle down to await our fate[141].

Tuesday 22nd August – An awful nights sleep is made worse by, I think, having too much sun yesterday resulting in a very bad headache and blurred vision. Still it could have been worse, at least we haven't been eaten by the beetle.

The alarm going off at 5:20am is a welcome relief to me as my headache and stomach cramps have meant I have been awake for a couple of hours already. There isn't the spectacular sunrise that we expected but at least its stopped raining after the thunderstorm in the night.

We leave the site by 6am and, whilst we have enjoyed our stay, think that it is unlikely we would return. It's been a great place to push the pause button on a trip like this to ake stock but now its back to the day job of travelling. Of course there is nowhere booked for tonight and as we head down the trail towards the ferry we are not even sure where we are going but we think the hours on the ferry will be a good time to plan.

By 6.30 we are at the terminal and the boat is already filling up, we choose a comfortable place at the back of the vessel where we can wedge our rucsacs in between the bench and the bulkhead. Then make ourselves comfortable ready for the 6.50 departure. Almost immediately we have to move the rucsacs so a very long electrical cable can be unplugged, I am about to explain to the crew that our rucsacs aren't so heavy that they will stop the electricity from flowing through the cable when I realise that the ferry has been *on charge* overnight and they are removing the cable from the boat[142].

---

[141] We hear no more from it.

Most of the passengers are crowding on the sunny side of the boat as it is a little chilly, we even have our fleeces on and one of the locals has a body warmer on so large that she looks as if she has been overinflated. This means that we are starting to tilt to one side so the crew are wandering up and down asking people to move to the other. They reluctantly do this.

At 6.50 on the nose we pull out into the Danube once more. Yes, the ferries can run on time in Romania, just not the trains. For the first ten minutes of the journey we move gingerly up the channel and I start to wonder if we are going to have a cursed fast ferry again[143]. My concerns are soon waylaid as we hit mid channel, the engines are brought up to full revs and we head back for Tulcea at top speed. Where we are sitting gives us a great view of the wake created by the ferry and the view back towards the Black Sea. However, it does smell of the engines which is not to everyone's taste and certainly not the family who up sticks and wonder off to find somewhere else.

Over the last few visits to Romania we have found that once people realise that we are English (it only takes one look at us to work this out) then people immediately start to treat us differently. I suppose that this is to be expected and is something that we accept with grace (probably something to do with us being English). This approach seems to manifest

---

[142] The cable resembles one that you may buy from B & Q and probably not safety tested but it is taken to shore so not our problem.

[143] Many years ago we took the Fast Ferry from Holyhead to Dun Laoghaire but the main engine (or something) broke about ten minutes out and we limped across the Irish Sea at the pace of a normal ferry.

itself in two distinct ways; Firstly, we are English and so, obviously, a tourist and they then choose to practice their English, try and find out about England etc. This leads to them being nicer than they may have otherwise have been so we say great things about them and buck the trend of people having a go at Romania. This makes travel nice and when you get chatting to people the whole journey passes more pleasantly. Secondly, and this applies across all nationalities, are those who feel that they are better than you and that you should move/comply to what they want. Thankfully this second type is quite rare and so when it does occur it is more of an irritant than a full blown annoyance. Today it is one of those days as we look out at the Danube over the bow of the boat. Our rucsacs are wedged into the space in front of our seats and we are, effectively, using them as footstools. This means that people cannot get across the deck using the gap in front of us. There is an audible "oh no!" from a couple of people who are horrified (not too strong a word) when they realise that they cannot step in front of our seats and spend the journey blocking our view – instead they are forced to skulk in a corner.

As the sun changes position, and the area of shade moves, then so do the smokers who have been loitering to our left. Our lungs thank them for this kind gesture as they head to the other side of the boat. The number moving doesn't appear to have affected the boat's performance.

I finish the biography of George Finch[144] concluding that the British team in 1922 deserved to fail climbing the Big Hill

---

[144] The Maverick Mountaineer: The Remarkable Life of George Ingle Finch: Climber, Scientist, Inventor

due to the type of people on the Everest Committee at the time. If they had listened to Finch before setting off in 1924 then they may have been more successful. Once more I digress.

We dock after about three and a half hours on the water, two hours quicker than the slow ferry and we were travelling against the current. Still it has been a long journey that we happily disembark from. As we get off we notice that someone has brought a motor scooter on board and is now waiting to disembark using a long, narrow, plank. Our departure is achieved by climbing around the back of another boat! It's not very elegant but at least it works.

Back on terra firma we go and get the train tickets for Constanta. We will have to change at Medgidia. Again this does not appear on our app, although a variation of it does so we conclude that it should be ok. It should get us in for about six but, once more, this is dependent on so many variables that we are just happy to be back in travelling mode. Walk down the prom in search of food and end up in the Cheers Bar for a couple of coffees. Back home it would be called a sports bar due to the huge television with tennis playing away. In front of the screen are a few locals who appear to have been there for some time judging by the number of glasses in front of them. Guinness is heavily advertised but there appears to be few local beers, is this the face of things to come?

With my birthday a few weeks away H decides that now is a good time to plan what to get me. Using the power of the internet (and free wifi) she does a bit of research before ordering to get me a food processor. The world seems a much smaller place. I order more coffee.

The sun is still out but a gentle breeze blowing across the Danube makes it much more tolerable. Oddly last year we left Tulcea when it was overcast and raining (here's hoping that the train is air conditioned). Leaving the Cheers Bar we walk back to the station calling in for a lemonade (best 'normal' one of the trip so far although Iasi still wins the prize with their mint lemonade) at a partially finished taverna type café next to the boat ticket office.

1pm and we head off for the train. As you would expect there is the usual chaos as people wrestle with their luggage before trying to find a seat. Somehow I manage to get H's rucsac on the rack above the seats in the middle of this madness whilst mine is wedged under our seats. We are in and comfortable (sort of). As soon as the train pulls out everyone on board starts to open their food parcels and consume lunch. We dine on pastry covered sausages and some sort of pretzel (although not the sort that are strung together) that H got from a local bakery after a classic bit Romanian queuing involving some rucsac jostling. Our view from this train is not hindered by the graffiti although there is some damage to one of the windows that appears to have had a brick thrown at it. More importantly the air conditioning works.

The early start means that we are both very tired and so sleep through the first section of the journey which is through the drab part of the countryside. Our slumbers are only broken by a domestic argument that is taking place. What about we don't know but it results in a rather large gentleman stomping off down the train away from his partner. About an hour later he returns, still stomping, grabs his gear and wanders off back towards First Class. He is still on his own. We have no idea what the argument was about but the guard appeared to be involved as both peace maker and chief agitator. I get out my Kindle and hide behind it[145].

We arrive in Medgidia about six minutes late (so, in Romanian train terms, on time) and together with lots of people get off and clutter up the platform like a group of people who have been travelling for four hours to get to the sales early. The final destination for the train we have got of is Bucharest but it looks as if most of us are heading for Constanta. For that we need a train. A large group of youths arrive on the platform and, together with their sub-woofer, head over to another part of the station. Everyone shares glances hoping that they are not heading for Constanta unsure if it has turned into the rave capital of Romania but no one has been told?

An elderly couple who appear to be interested in the station but not the trains, as they don't seem to be getting on one of them, approach us and ask us if we are going to Constanta. When we say yes they make a big effort to point us in the right direction. We had already worked this out but it makes them happy (and we are happy of the confirmation) so we accept the instructions and head for Platform 2. Beyond our platform, on Platform 4, we notice the youth group, with the sub-woofer, are waiting for the train back towards Tulcea so

---

[145] In days gone by it was easy to bury your face in a book in order to hide from someone's gaze. Hiding behind a tablet or e-reader doesn't seem so easy.

we have to conclude that they are heading for one of the minor stations that we went through on the way south[146].

H buys us both ice cream, mine is an old fashioned ice cream sandwich and is surprisingly good (surprising because the wrapper makes it look less than appetizing). H has a more traditional lolly and then wanders off to look at the canal which is down the road from the station and returns with stories of feral dogs wandering around. I go down a few moments later but see none, only lots of derelict building typical of the area around a station.

I return to look after the rucsacs whilst this time H heads off over the steps over the tracks to see what lies beyond the marshalling area (actually it's a large area that looks like a train graveyard) and finds a large Gypsy camp. As she returns I set off camera in hand to investigate. I manage to get a few photographs of the resting rolling stock before I hear a familiar voice shouting across the tracks, "Gary!". Its obvious that our train is about to arrive so I abandon the photoshoot and hot foot it back to our platform where H has her rucsac on but there is no sign of the train. She did try to give me the "Don't rush, its ok" signal (whatever that is) but I missed it and arrived back at the platform out of breath.

Our link to Constant arrives at 4:57 and leaves at 4;59. Due to our current position in the game of Romanian Train Roulette we have no idea where the train has come from, where it stops along the way or anything. All we know is that we are heading east (we have a compass) and that

---

[146] Many of the minor stations only appear to be served by the trains heading north so in some cases it is necessary to travel all the way to Medgidia then out again.

Constanta is 36km away (easy internet check). Still at least we are moving.

Two stops later and we grind to a halt at Basarabi for what appears to be a cigarette stop (for both passengers and staff) or maybe its because we are ahead of the fictitious schedule that we are following (although I doubt it). Still, it gives us another chance to watch how quickly people can disembark, smoke a cigarette and get back onto a train (is this an Olympic event?). H moves over to the other side of the train to get a better view of the river/canal but as the train sets off again soon finds herself looking at the retaining wall. At least its started to get a little cooler.

Most of the stations on the way have water towers from the old days of steam and it is interesting to see how the styles change from place to place, presumably depending on what materials were available, how much time was available and the skill of the builder. This varies from nice looking brick ones that have been well maintained through to crumbling Communist concrete which have had no maintenance and are on the verge of collapse. We tick off the stations and even try and work out our speed using the kilometre markers by the side of the tracks.

Constanta station is a mess, especially for a large town. It has none of the charm of the other stations we have been to, nor any redeeming features. To make it even worse there is a lot of building work being done. The underpass that takes you between the platforms is dark and forbidding and the sealing off of the tunnel at one end using tarpaulin doesn't help. The ramp up to the front of the main building does make it is little easier before we go outside and are immediately pounced upon by people offering us taxi services. There is even a bloke we saw on the platform waving his keys at me offering me a lift. But we have decided to walk anyway, its only half an hour[147], we have been stuck inside all day, it's a nice evening and (most importantly) its cool.

Type our destination into Google Maps and try and get away from the front of the station which is clogged up with the usual collection of taxis, maxicabs, minibuses and coaches as they manoeuvre like some sort of mobile Tetris as they tout their trade. No one can move in any direction. Come on Constanta, if you want people to visit then get this sorted out, remember that first impressions count. As always I make a mental note to write to the tourist board.

On the first section of the walk we are *joined* by two exceptionally jolly teenagers who are just laughing at everything and generally being happy with the world. They peel off and head into the local park still giggling after about fifteen minutes, presumably heading for some open mike comedy club. We soon discover that the drivers are as bad here as they are in Bucharest but they don't have the advantage of wide boulevards to swerve into when things go wrong. The upshot of this is that we see lots of dented cars and the side of the road is littered with car parts!

The Hotel Voila, where we are staying is at the other end of the town from the station near the marina and whilst it is a

---

[147] As with many timings those given by some of the accommodations assume that (1) you know where you are going, (2) you can power walk and (3) you are not carrying your own body weight on your back!

long and pleasant walk it is a little more than the promised thirty minutes. The final section is, however, downhill.

Bookings.com describes it as "quirky in a Moorish way" and this is certainly the case with narrow corridors and staircases going off at various points. Some of the staircases appear to not go anywhere but are just put there for show. We book in and, for the first time in the trip, Newby Cat hardly raises a smile from the receptionist who informs us that we have been upgraded to a Junior Suite, with a jacuzzi, at no extra charge. Another bonus is that the room is on the ground floor thus meaning that we don't have to carry the rucsacs up the narrow stairs for, whilst I am sure there is a lift, we can see no sign of it.

The room is very quirky and a very odd shape. At one end of the huge bedroom area there is a small raised section as if a small stage, on which is a small table and two chairs. Unfortunately, in order to manoeuvre the chairs and sit down, it requires a delicate balancing act so that the chairs do not fall off the *stage*. The high ceilings give the owners the chance to display some rather spectacular wall hangings that, while not being of my choosing, do suit the room very well. The bathroom is tucked away and reached via a step and two sets of doors. The jacuzzi bath doesn't disappoint but as we expect, when turned on, it floods the bathroom.

Hits of the 1980s on the TV. It is unclear if they are just a random shuffle of numbers or whether they are trying to put them in some sort of ranked order. It's a great trip down memory lane although I'm not sure if Lionel Ritchie's lecturer in *Hello* would have kept his job (obviously they were different times). Oh yes and the lovely Lysette

Anthony appears in lots of videos. Washed and change we head out in search of food.

From the hotel if we turn right and head up the hill we get to the Old Town, to the left and we will head to the marina area. We head left and I find myself in my worst nightmare, lots of *posh* restaurants where everyone else is well dressed and I look like I've just travelled down from the Delta on a raft. The food at all of these eateries looks excellent but they all seem to be selling 'non-native' dishes. I want to run up to the waiters, point at the Black Sea and shout "Fish!" but as H points out they probably wouldn't understand and would just offer me a pizza.

We go from restaurant to restaurant examining the menus (think we go to twelve) before we return to one[148] that offers a fish dish that H fancies. Of course, when we try and order it we discover that they don't have it. At least the beer is local[149]. We order a couple and send the waitress off on another lap whilst H ploughs through the menu again for something else finally settling on a dish with anchovies (lots of them). I do my usual speed ordering and have that local Romania delicacy of fajitas. The table next to us is hosting some sort of family gathering. H fascinates a small girl on the end of the table and she waves. My face pulling routine doesn't seem to appeal as much and she eventually goes back to the party. With a little effort we work out the WIFI password and H gets to work doing some research on what we must see while we are here[150]. I have the pleasure of the

---

[148] The Reyna
[149] One of the other bars only sells Stella.
[150] Our usual approach is typing in 'Ten things to do in .....'. Invariably this brings up at least five things that are not possible/have been

company of lots of small children who are trying to sell me more roses than is really necessary – I try to explain that I much prefer the mixed bouquet from Morrisons but it falls on deaf ears. Fed and watered H declines anything else to eat here suggesting that we get an ice cream on the way back by heading back into the Old Town. This involves climbing some rather impressive stairs that are far grander than is necessary for where they are positioned and then through some rather crumbly alleyways into the main square.

The Old Town is extremely busy but remembering the Romanians love of promenading it is not really a surprise. All of the bars and cafes are heaving but what we can't find is an ice cream stand (usually they are everywhere) and so we end up at the smallest mini market we have been to so far. The size of a small cupboard it sells beer and ice cream, both of which are in padlocked fridges. We opt for the ice cream and make our way through the streets of Constanta to the hotel where we discover that it is a countdown of the best of the Eighties and Michael Jackson's Billy Jean is at number one. H lays on the bed and promptly falls asleep.

Wednesday 23rd August – I awake a little after 7 and, despite the best efforts of the World Service, can't go back to sleep so its Kindle time. H slumbers on until 9.30 before I have the nerve to wake her up by playing Fur Elise slowly increasing the volume until she emerges from her cocoon.

Breakfast at the Voila is a confusing affair as it is served on the roof terrace. Challenge One is to get there as we have to work out which of the sets of stairs to use before emerging

---

knocked down or are too expensive!

in the middle of the breakfast area. Challenge Two is whether we sit inside or outside. It's a nice morning so outside it on a snug balcony with spectacular views over towards the Black Sea. The waitress has little English and the three of us struggle to work out what is/isn't as part of the buffet. What we do manage to do is order omelette and coffee. H wanders off to wrestle with the toast machine while I take in the view.

One black coffee arrives with a glass of milk on the side, something obviously got lost in translation. Knowing how the system works we immediately order two more coffees and feel sad that there is no *resident operated* coffee machine as many hotels appear to be adopting. H returns with freshly made toast and comments on how easy the machine is to use (its not a normal toaster but more of a Heath Robinson toasting machine that gives the bread the full, immersive, toast experience rather than just toasting both sides).

The omelettes are nice and thick (not your one egg omelette here) and very tasty.

From the roof we have views over to the Black Sea as well as back towards the town (although our position means that the Old Town is out of sight over the brow). Near to us the buildings are definitely in need of some much needed restoration although several appear to have already had work started on them. Beyond them we can see the new apartments that are going up around the edge of the marina[151].

---

[151] During our stay we don't see any work being carried out on the apartment complex at all, even though tower cranes are in situ.

Breakfast consumed and it's back to the room for a quick tidy up and then some research on Scatman John (after Ski Ba Bop Ba Dop Bop came on the music channel). All our gear, which had previously been strewn around the room after the rucsacs were just emptied on arrival, is now safely stowed as we have drawers and a wardrobe.

We decide to start our tour of the town by heading down to the harbour and marina area which is a lot quieter than it was last night. Between the boats, none of which look cheap we can see various forms of marine life swimming around in the green murky depths. From here not only is the Ukraine accessible (at the other side of the Black Sea) but turning right out of the harbour will get you to Bulgaria, then Turkey so we can see why all of the boats are well kitted out for long journeys. On the far harbour wall there are what look like Henry Moore style toadstools which we discover are to stop erosion of the coast (although they could also pass for anti-tank devices).

At the corner of the harbour we walk up to the old lighthouse and what looks like old Naval barracks. The latter is all closed up and appears to be the subject of a major piece of renovation. With its close proximity to the apartment block we wonder if it is being incorporated into that. All the area is fenced off so close inspection is not possible and a couple of little dogs on the other side make their presence known by barking incessantly when I try and sneak through.

We now have the biggest surprise of the day (the bear is probably the biggest surprise of the trip) as we round the corner and look down the coast we see the Casino. The surprise of seeing this is similar to when they discover the Statue of Liberty at the end of Planet of the Apes[152]. There, at the other end of the boulevard is Constanta Casino a superb piece of architecture which dominates the headland. Sadly whilst in a much better state than the one in Piatra Neamt it is still fenced off and in desperate need of investment to save it from a slow decay.

Considering its glamorous history[153] it seems odd that now it's only occupants appear to be pigeons and a cat. At the far end a section is being used as a TV/film set with the several large vans parked outside declaring their involvement (the sign painting giving it away that they are catering etc).

---

[152] Spoiler alert. I mean the Charlton Heston version from 1968
[153] Built in 1910 it paid host to the Russian Royal Family in 1914

There is an open door into the Casino where a few people are trying to walk in and I start to follow them before a, rather large, security man steps forward saying "Nu!" in a very direct way. Tempted though I am to say that I am with the BBC I conclude that retreat is the best option and wander back to find that H has climbed down to the beach but returns saying that it "smells of wee!". Having tried, unsuccessfully, to squeeze through the fence to get a better photograph of the building we step back and find a man fitting a new handle to his fork. When I say handle I mean just a piece of wood that he was trying to shape in a *make do and mend* way. We hope that one day the building will be repaired/renovated along the same lines of the one in Cluj.

Opposite the casino is an aquarium with two pages of rules posted on the door as we go in (in English and Romanian and including the ubiquitous "no cycling" rule which appears to be in place in all Romanian museums). Its not as good as the one in Tulcea and has, mainly, non-local fish, many being from the Amazon. But at 10RON each it's well worth it and has an excellent one-way system.

We walk back into the Old Town navigating using only a rough sense of direction and occasional glances of the churches. On the way we walk past some Roman ruins[154] which appear to have been taken over by many of the local homeless people who have made some quite substantial bivouacs amongst the rocks. I'm not sure what seems the oddest, the open air Roman ruins with no fence around them or the people sleeping amongst them.

---

[154] Roman ruins are very common in Constanta to the point of them being too common.

We pass the mosque and emerge into one of the many squares that the town is built around, complete with the ubiquitous Roman ruins scattered about. Beyond it we stop off at the Arabian Coffee Shop where the Rough Guide promises us good food and drinks with *miserable service*. In a country where we have found this sort of service everywhere we decide this is a must and are a little disappointed to find that the staff are extremely friendly and welcoming. We are then faced with the coffee menu which to say the least is very complex and confusing with us being given such a vast choice of different types of bean, then different type of roast and so on. I plump for an iced latte which has a title that is much more impressive than the actual product. H has a much more refreshing iced tea with ginger (good choice in a coffee shop). A, presumably local, small dog wanders over to the café where it is petted by one of the waitresses and we wonder if it does belong to them. What is clear is that it has very impressive ears that flap around rather similar to those of Dumbo. Looking around we realise that many of the buildings have a Moorish style, obviously influenced by the traders who have been using this port since Roman times[155].

We are told that a visit to Constanta isn't complete unless you have climbed the minaret of the Grand Mosque (or Marea Moschee din Constanţa or Carol I Mosque) so back across the square we find the entrance, which is not obvious, and having paid the 4RON entry go inside. A simple list of rules are shown as we enter the Prayer Hall, the key one of which is not to take photographs so the camera is put in the

---

[155] It is the largest port on the Black Sea and one of the largest in Europe.

bag. We are restricted from going into the main area by a rope barrier which I find quite reassuring as it stops many people disrespectfully wandering around[156]. Now for the minaret. Its a long climb up a constant left hand spiral staircase that is so unremitting that we almost feet motion sick, it is certainly very disorienting. On the plus side at least it is wide enough to allow people to pass without having to snuggle too much up against the wall. At the top of the spirals the final, metal, section of stairs resembles of rather cobbled together teenager welding project that takes us to the outside balcony through a doorway that was made for someone who was under five feet tall. So, I am out on the ledge. Am I ok? Well, if I keep my back to the wall and look straight out then I am. If I look down then maybe not so. A large speaker is bolted to the outside at *bang head level* and I'm pretty sure that no one wants to be out here when that is on calling people to prayer. The views from here are excellent looking over the crumbling roof tops towards the Black Sea.

Back down the stairs, as confusing going down as they were going up, we leave the mosque and head for the town museum. After the pleasantness of the people at the café and the mosque we are taken aback as we are faced with ex-Communist efficiency in the guise of a grumpy cashier. The problem is our fault as we try and pay with a 100RON note. From inside her hermetically sealed (probably) bubble she starts waving her arms and gesturing to the other notes that we have. We need 26RON but, in loose *noteage*, we only have 24. We count it out in front of her to prove the point

---

[156] I am finding that the more I travel the more I find my respect for other people's different religious beliefs increases and the thought of just tramping through such as place of worship scares me.

but still the gesticulations continue. We offer her 116RON suggesting that she could give us 90RON change in the form of a 50RON and a couple of 20RON notes. Still there is the arm waving before she, rather reluctantly, accepts our offer. The cash drawer is then opened to reveal that she has a plentiful supply of change, such is Romanian efficiency. We go into the museum.

Most of the museum is put over to the origins of the town and the archaeological digs that have taken place. As we have discovered, around every corner there are Roman remains and the museum has a detailed street maps showing evidence of this. Even better is that most of the descriptions are also in English. As with all the museums we have visited we have a shadow who follows us making sure that we don't steal anything (although how we could walk off with a Roman Column does pose an interesting question). We give her the slip after about fifteen minutes when she spies another couple who must look dodgier than us. Up a level, and now free to wander, we have more displays about Tomis (as Constanta was called in Roman times). Sadly at this point the signs in English run out and we are left trying to guess what the photos and dates represent. The top floor has a substantial exhibition about Communism in Romania, something that almost thirty years after the death of Nicolae Ceaușescu the country is still struggling to come to terms with. Again the information boards are in Romanian but looking at the dates we work out that the Danube Canal was, effectively, dug using slave labour[157]. It was quite a sobering

---

[157] We subsequently found out that over a million political prisoners were used in the project using poor quality equipment that had been used by the Russians on the Volga Don Canal. The result of this was that much of it was dug using picks and shovels.

exhibit and many of the Romanians who were there spent a considerable amount of time going through the archives.

We leave the museum and head straight back into the heat for whilst there was no air conditioning in the museum the thickness of the walls meant that it was reasonably cool. Time for lunch and we head off to try and find the Byblos which is recommended in the Rough Guide as an excellent place to dine (and no mention of miserable staff). This involves leaving the Old Town and heading off on the main road, that appears to link the Old with the New, near the park that our comedic friends had hidden in yesterday. A section of car bonnet graces the pavement obviously evidence of a recent altercation. There is no sign of the rest of the car!

Our original thought was to sit outside but when we arrive we realise that it is on a, very, main road (with poor air quality) we opt for the air conditioned splendour of the interior. We enter to one of the warmest welcomes we have had of the trip so far and are given the choice of several tables. One section is taped off presumably for this evening's action and we have the usual wander around trying to find the 'right place'. Finally settling on a central table where H has a good view of the comings and goings of the customers and staff.

The food is excellent, although the waiter is thrown by my request for some polenta to go with the Lebanese Sausages (what can I say? I like polenta!). When the sausages arrive they come with a lot of freshly baked bread (about half a loaf) so I can understand his surprise at my request as I have a complete carbohydrate overload.

We discuss how this place is in the Rough Guide, what is the criteria for appearing in it? There is no doubt that it is a very good place to eat but in no way can it be put at the budget end of the market (that you would expect for an 'impoverished hitchhiker trying to get by on.....'[158]) and an unwary traveller may find their budget seriously damaged or totally blown.

Once more in the trip I develop a blinding headache which H puts down to dehydration and orders a jug of water for me. I drink it, another arrives, then a third all of which I consume. Our, very helpful, waiter becomes a veritable Aquarius as he ferries supplies from the kitchen to our table. It is only afterwards that we think he may have thought that there was something wrong with the food, hence the excessive helpfulness. As the place is, relatively, empty we use the opportunity to plan for tomorrow. More water is drunk and I feel a lot better. As we leave we can sense the waiter punching the air as he has saved a life!

Within ten minutes of leaving we encounter two wonderful Romanian quirks. Firstly we pass a betting shop where it appears that smoking is banned in the building. On the door is a fly screen consisting of long, extremely colourful, ribbons. As we approach a hand appears through the screen with a cigarette on the end of it. Then a head pokes through, quickly smokes the cigarette, and goes back inside. At no time does any other part of his body breach the screen.

---

[158] With a nod to Douglas Adams

The second Romanian quirk is a statue to the 1989 Revolution. It is overgrown with vegetation and appears to have been built on the collapsed plinth of an old statue. Oh yes and it has two people, sort of, fastened together. Very weird, very quirky and very Romanian.

We wander out of town towards the University where we suspect we can get down to the beach. Sadly there is no obvious way and it takes us some time to find steps that head in the right direction, i.e. towards the Sea. At the bottom we find what at first appears to be soft sand but on closer inspection is mainly shingle, miles of it with a poorly maintained walkway across some sections.

Depending on your view point it's now either late in the afternoon or early in the evening. Either way the beach is, relatively, devoid of people. We can't say empty as there are several hundred sunbeds all neatly lined up in large blocks ready for tomorrow's customers. A few of these show some signs of occupation, that is they are towelled, and we guess that they belong to the handful of people who are in the Sea.

Between the sunbeds and the Sea is a woman doing Yoga (clothed) looking towards Crimea about 400 kilometres away (yes, the Black Sea is that big!). At the moment it certainly is a great place to meditate and contemplate life, although I suspect that during the day it may be a little livelier! We make our way towards the harbour breakwater to investigate the pre-cast concrete 'anti-tank' blocks[159] that it is constructed from; there are hundreds of them that appear to have been just stacked to construct the marina basin. As we climb onto the breakwater, taking a short cut across the blocks H slips and plants herself in the water. Wet shorts but otherwise unhurt, at first I am a little worried that she may have hurt her ankle again[160] but when she voices her concern over her phone getting wet, which was in her bag, then I knew she was ok.

As we walk along the breakwater we see a rather overloaded pirate styled boat heading out of the marina with what appears to be a party on board. Initially we are rather concerned that the boat is heading out into the Black Sea, in the early evening, with a drunk group of passengers on board. But then spot that it is turning around before the end

---

[159] We subsequently find out that they are called Tetra-pods and are very popular in Japan.
[160] A long standing, old running injury.

of the wall and appears to be doing a ten minute waltz around the harbour area rather than a full on assault on Odessa. The passengers continue to wave and shout to us as they head back in. We politely wave back.

A drink is called for and so we head back to the marina thinking that we can have a sit and a quiet beer. Sadly the drinks companies have other ideas and we have a choice of Carlsberg or Stella! Make our way back up to the Old Town which, by this time, is coming to life which lots of people out and about. A quick reconnaissance tells us that the only bars that look reasonable are playing loud music. Back to our favourite kiosk (cupboard) for a couple of cans and head back to the room to try and use the jacuzzi (no mean feat as it involves flooding the bathroom again).

Thursday 22nd August – GCSE Results Day back home. I wish I could say that H woke up naturally to the sound of the birds singing outside the room but its not the case as Herb Alpert's Casino Royale blares out from the phone alarm. She doesn't move so I walk around to her side and turn it off. Give her a bit more time before putting the television on, only then does she start to stir. But even then it's only to complain about the news being on so early. She slowly emerges from under the duvet.

First adventure of the day is to head up (the correct stairs) to the restaurant. After yesterday's issues we have worked out what to do and order most things on the menu although the poached eggs appear to be fried and the coffee, again, takes ages to arrive. Because of the coffee delay we initially decide not to order a second but the waitress has other ideas and appears with two more coffees as she anticipates our needs. We sit back down, enjoy the coffee and continue to watch the world go by. A medieval drama (Romanian) plays to itself on the television in the corner.

Despite the heat we decide that it's a good idea to head out to the Dolphinarium and, remembering yesterday's headache, decide that lots of water is required and fill up our bottles accordingly. Then it's to reception and the traditional fun of ordering a taxi. This tradition normally includes the discussion about where we are going, is it worth seeing and why are we here anyway! Today is no exception as we chat away with the receptionist who is loving practicing her English.

Taxi arrives and tries, unsuccessfully, to do a sort of power slide outside the hotel into the parking space. Its looks like it's going to be an exciting ride! For the first time in the trip I find myself sitting behind the driver (a privilege normally reserved by H so she can easily give instructions and lunge forward when necessary). As I shuffle across into place I realise that we have another, almost, horizontal driver and as we set off I realise that with a little effort I could massage his scalp with my thighs (I don't).

We head north towards the Dolphinarium at the usual speed used by the taxi drivers of Romania. I am a little concerned about his ability to see the road as I am pretty sure that I have the best view as I have no driver to block my vision and think he may be able to see the bottom of the steering wheel but that is all.
More by luck than anything (five near misses) we complete our most expensive taxi journey of the trip so far, at 25RON that roughly equates to a pound per near miss. A distance of

about six kilometres. As spectacularly as he arrived at the hotel our driver pulls up outside Dolphinarium, we pay our fare and, while trying not to squeeze his head with my legs, I get out.

The Dophinarium and Wild Life Park are two separate attractions with a joint ticket for them being 40RON but you have to book for the dolphins and the next show isn't until 3pm (its about 10am when we arrive). The cashier speaks little English but it is clear from her facial expression that she doesn't really think that its worth the wait, "Do you just want to go round the Park? Eez very good", so we hand over 16RON and in we go.

The Wild Life Park gets the thumbs up for the amount of shade that we are offered as we wander around although I think that many of the animals would have liked a little more as many of them are wedged into their huts to get out of the sun. Much of the ground is parched quite badly and, looking around, it appears that most of their food has been brought in as there is little grass. In fact the only animals that seem really happy are the birds who are splashing around in the river that goes through the Park. However, having seen the wild pelicans in the Delta, these don't quite cut it.

As we walk around the park H comes across a small girl who is about to push her finger into the raccoon's cage, where the residents look very hungry and excitable, and just manages to pull her away before it is bitten off (mum wasn' t quick enough to leap in and is grateful for H's assistance). Unfortunately we are not quick enough to stop a swan snapping at another child. No contact is made but she will carry the shock for some time, she is still crying about ten minutes later.

Guinea pigs and red squirrels are bunked in together in the same enclosure and seem to have established some sort of agreement as to who controls which part of the apparatus. This agreement is shown as we watch the guinea pigs try to climb up a ladder to the higher (squirrel) level. Here they are met by one of the squirrels who just pushes them off, they drop to the bottom of the enclosure and then start again. This seems to be happening on a delayed loop as different guinea pigs try and run the gauntlet but without success.

After a couple of hours of wandering around we pause for a coffee at the most hidden café we have ever visited, it is down a track off a main track etc. You get the impression that they don't want anyone to visit it! We get the map out in an effort to get oriented. Around the corner from the park is a wooden church that is on the 'must see' list whilst we are here. We can see it from the edge of the park but there is no direct access so its out of the park, back to the main road, past McDonalds, past all the litter from McDonalds (there is a lot), past some road works that to get round we have to walk out into the road before heading back by the side of a large lake that feeds the river through the park and finally we are there.

The wooden church is a very odd building where Scandinavian Wood meets Orthodox Church, built in 1990 it has a large open area which presumably has chairs when a service is on. Local radio music blasts out of the speakers that are positioned around the walls, which is certainly not what we expected. There are tables and chairs set up outside as if it offers teas and coffees but, sadly, it doesn't and after a bit of a wander around we head out.

Whilst in the area we feel we should have a wander around this end of town (which we have dubbed 'The New Bit') and walk around the edge of the lake where we find ourselves at the City Park Shopping Mall. This is exactly the same as all o the other malls in Romania, a style that appears to be taking over. We even spot a place nearby where we can buy gas. Into the mall we go and find a Paul's Patisserie similar to the one we had been to in Bucharest. H has a lemonade and I go for a frappe that, to be honest, is a little too.....well.....coffeey. It is very strong and after drinking it I wonder if I will ever sleep again. Still the air conditioning in the cafe is working well and we have enough wifi to start to plan our next move.

As we sit there a man walks in wearing a white lab coat and carrying an iPad as if it were a clipboard. He has a puzzled look on his face and talks, briefly, to the waitress. Then he has a quick look around, nods to the waitress and leaves. Not sure what they were being checked for but it would appear that they have passed whatever it was.

After a little discussion we decide to have a walk around the mall, firstly because it is air conditioned (it's still very hot outside) and secondly we need a toilet. There are signposts for the latter but finding it involves completing a couple of laps before we spot it down one of the many passageways that cut through the complex. On the plus side, during our laps, we notice a supermarket underneath the mall and so head there next to try, unsuccessfully, to buy some shaving paste similar to the tube I had bought back in 2015 (good travelling size). Sadly end up compromising with the Nivea version. Leaving the supermarket we discover that the mall is far bigger than we first thought (it is on multiple levels) and, having got a little lost, H spends some time having a look at the clothes before we try and get back on track and leave[161].

After a little more wandering we find our way out. It's an odd building as, at various times, we can see the outside but cannot get there. Eventually, we find a car on a display. Concluding that this must have been brought in from somewhere we try and retrace how we would have brought a car in and follow that route out. Our cunning scheme works and eventually we are outside and following the advice of Trip Advisor decide to try and find Tropaeum Traiani[162] which we understand is quite close. We load up the co-ordinates given and set off in search of a large grassed park area with a large, Roman, monument. Of course it's not going to be that easy.

We set off walking through various areas of Constanta that certainly aren't on the tourist map but they are going in 'the right direction' so who are we to argue. After some time, and a lot of road crossing, we are in Adamcisi. Which according to everything we have is where the monument is. It is not! We appear to be in a different Adamcisi and the one we want is several hours away (if we have a car), make a note to write to TripAdvisor. By this time H has had enough of wandering around, we are both hot and tired, so head back towards the shopping mall and, behind a Lidl locate a taxi rank.

---

[161] Throughout our trips H will always have a look at what is available, although most of the time she doesn't buy anything.
[162] This is a Roman monument built in 109 over some battle or other.

Start the clock – its time for Romanian Taxi Roulette.......

Taxi 1
Us: "Hello, Constanta?"
Driver: "No, I'm not taking"

Taxi 2
Us: "Hello, Constanta?"
Driver: "No, toiletten....." We are not sure if this means that
he has been to the toilet, was about to go to the toilet or he
thought that Constanta was a toilet. What we clear is that he
would not take us.

Taxi 3
Us: "Hello, Constanta?"
Driver: "Of course......where?"
Us: "Hotel Voila"
Driver: "Do you have GPS?"
Me: "Yes", I promptly wedge my phone on the dashboard, we
have found a new friend. As we drive at a rather sedate
speed towards the hotel (due to the traffic) we have a
commentary from the driver. This mainly involves him
shouting "zeees eez terribeeel!" and gesturing to the other
drivers, using both hands. Best driver so far.

We are dropped off close to the Voila as there are road
works and make our way to our room to watch Bones. Wake
up half an hour later – its beach time.

H has given a lot of thought about how we can go to the
beach with the minimum of gear so we are not leaving things
lying around (we have no intention of hiring a sun lounger!).
In the end we go with putting some money in the waterproof

Hagloff pouch we have and a towel around our shoulders. Off we go walking past the numerous cats that frequent the area around the hotel.

The water is nowhere near as warm as the Delta and the pouch fails as we have not fastened it properly so we have soggy cash. Apart from that a late afternoon swim is certainly welcome but after about 40 minutes we are bored and head back to the hotel, maybe some waves might have made it a little more interesting.

Naked Gun is on the television as we get sorted and changed ready to head out. This time we decide to turn right out of the hotel and up to the Old Town where H has set her eyes on the Pizzero in the town square. We hover around the entrance as it's packed and we try to work out if there is space inside. Whilst hovering we are approached by one of the waiters who beckons us in (Cuic Weizan is on draught so in we go). Once more we think that they find a space for us as we are English and I am carrying a notebook, maybe a TripAdvisor sticker on the notebook next time.

My first pasta choice is not available so end up with Salmon Tagliatelle, H has the mixed fish stew which she describes as 'soupy stew'. Both are very tasty and well presented. After the meal two very well dressed men approach us advertising a new beer, would I like to try it? I explain that I am English but love Romanian beers and our son works for a brewery in the UK. This qualifies me for a couple of free glasses[163]. They film me saying how much I like the beer and this involvement with the product leads to lots of people in the

---

[163] Thanks Tom.

restaurant happily volunteering to take part. Almost a 'look, the English bloke is involved so it must be good!'[164]. From where we are we have a clear view looking towards the square where they are starting the construction of a stage and gantries ready some sort of concert. Health and Safety risks are, obviously, looked at very carefully as the workers climb the half built scaffolding carrying more scaffolding poles.

The TV at one end of the restaurant (yes, I know it's odd) has the hunting and fishing channel playing away to itself with a programme about shooting wild boar and catching fish in an 'urban' river (although I think the word that might be used is sewer!).

We order pudding and wait.......... In fact we are waiting so long that we speculate that no-one has previously ordered one and so they are looking for a recipe.

A trip to the toilet here is an adventure in itself as the circuitous route that we have to take passes the freezers that have cow carcases hanging up and it's a bit like walking through a Damien Hearst retrospective. From here it's a mountain trek up the stairs, the route is so long that, by the time you got back to the table, it was almost time to set off back again.

As an aside, we have noticed that many Romanian women spend a lot of money on shoes. Fortunately most of them fall into the 'sensible' or 'comfortable' category rather than heels and so are well suited for the poorly maintained pavements,

---

[164] It was very nice

cobbled street and pot holes. Thus it is a surprise to witness two ladies walk in with extremely high heels (five plus inches). After saying that the word 'walk' is used with some reservation, as they seemed to be just trying to stand upright and any forward propulsion was somewhere between difficult and impossible (and involved grabbing hold of chairs, walls etc in order to not fall down).

Eventually my Papanași arrives, it is very nice and well worth the wait. The delay in it being brought gives us a welcome opportunity to do some people watching. It's big enough to feed two people but H declines eating some of mine having consumed her ice cream. 176RON (about £35) for a meal for two, including drinks, that was fit for a king!

Before leaving the restaurant I make one last visit to the toilet once more saying hello to the carcasses. One of the gentlemen in the toilets is making sounds not dissimilar to what I think would be overheard during a hernia operation but as I lack any real medical training I didn't hang around.

The sun had set some time ago so we decide to wander over to the casino to see if it is floodlit in an evening as we had seen some photographs suggesting that. As we walk past the Naval building and lighthouse we can hear music, a combination of piano accordion and opera singing. We soon meet the source of the sound as we follow other people walking along the promenade towards the casino. Here we find that the lovely café culture has spread and we find a group of opera singers (complete with a grand piano) performing as part of the Festivalul de Arta Tomisul Etern which has been running at various sites around Constanta for the past few days. There are eight singers, four sopranos and four tenors, performing extracts from various operas handing the microphone around where necessary, although am pretty sure that they don't really need it. This is all taking place in front a flood lit casino, what an absolutely spectacular sight. Hairs stand up on the back of my neck as they sing The Drinking Song from La Traviata as a finale and plastic cups of wine are passed around the audience.

And then its all over and to think that if I'd gone back to the hotel for the better camera I'd have missed all this. A few of the performers wander off but the main bulk all line up for photos and are happy to chat to the members of the audience. A girl of about eight or nine sits at the piano and starts to play exquisitely, without sheet music. This is the background music as we head back towards the marina to try and get a drink, this is mainly to take away the flavour of the wine we have just had (although it was a lovely gesture). The marina bars are either heaving or have closed for the night so we head back to the hotel.

On the television is an episode of NCIS that I've seen before (the one with the computer hacker who they pretend they are going to send to Guantanamo Bay). H falls asleep.

Friday 25th August – early, for us, breakfast on the roof. We vary our choice again with H hoping to have a grapefruit and the meat/cheese platter. Of course it doesn't arrive so she has half of my omelette. At least lots of coffee is brought over as they get used to us.

The plan, such as it is, is to spend the morning in Constanta doing a trawl of the Roman sites we have missed and then head to Bucharest mid-afternoon (there is a train at 2pm).

We don't have to be out of the hotel until noon so we can leave our gear in the room rather than messing with left luggage.

We head back to the town centre (now we know the way) and have a good look at all of the Roman sarcophagi that are almost scattered around the square as if the attitude of the council is "Oh look, another one. Just put it over there!" – so many in fact that I joke to H that I wonder if they use them as litter bins. Then promptly remove a Radler can from one of them and place it in the bin that is less than two metres away. I wonder what the Romans would say?

Every so often we come across plaques giving information about the various ruins, some of which are in English but all of which appear to be obituaries to the seems odd).

Next stop at the end of the square is a huge Temple of Brutalism which surrounds the Roman Mosaic[165] that is largely intact. The building itself reminds us of a late 1960s/early 1970s leisure centre complete with a concrete roof that looks as if it was cast in one section and lots and lots of glass added to the sides. Unlike most of the buildings like this in the UK that have been demolished this shrine to concrete is being maintained by patching it up to keep most of the water out. Not pretty but extremely practical. The route round the mosaic is well signposted (lots of keep off signs) but then, suddenly, it goes outside (its difficult to understand why and even more difficult to explain) and along a delightful concrete balcony[166]. We look towards the

---

[165] Discovered in 1959
[166] Delightful to a fan of Brutalism

docks that make Constanta so important then, glancing down, we see what appears to be a lot of re-enactment groups starting to set up for a weekend of Roman stuff. After saying that their tents look a little more medieval than we would have expected. They have also brought in a lot of straw bails. The signposted tour now takes us back inside where we get up close and personal(ish) with the mosaic itself and we can't help commenting that with a little more effort it could be a whole lot better (sadly this would require a considerable amount of investment of money that the country doesn't have).

Back outside once more we loop around the museum and drop down to the encampment below, no easy task as we have to weave in and out of more Roman ruins (many pieces have been heavily graffitied). The re-enactors are just setting everything up for the week and so are very surprised to see a couple of tourists wandering past their tents looking at the half set up stalls selling jewellery, sweets and cakes. They are even more surprised when they realise that we are British. We fall into conversation with someone who, of course, asks 'Why are you here?'. They are then surprised when we laugh.

More Roman ruins are passed as we climb up a grassy bank to get a better view over towards the main dock area which is absolutely packed with large container vessels. The sheer size of the docks area is spectacular. Towards the edge of it we spot the old Maritime Rail Station that looks as elegant as any of the stations that we have seen in Romania but, sadly, is not accessible due to the heavy security that surrounds it. Dropping down we walk out onto a promontory that encases a large car park that looks as if it should have a restaurant at the end[167]. What it does have are a lot of learner drivers who are taking it in turns to practice, there are even traffic cones for them to weave in and out of. The promontory has its fair share of the large concrete Tetrapods that we have come to accept in the area together with a large, concrete, wall that we climb onto to get better views looking north towards the casino.

Walking back along the main promenade we pass a half constructed restaurant/hotel which has large signs announcing the opening of it in 2018.

Outside the casino all evidence of the opera performance has been removed (even the grand piano) and, in its place, a basketball court has been set up complete with artificial grass presumably for some weekend event that is taking place. Advertising hoardings are being carried in as we pass.

Pause by the Naval College for the view. Here work is being carried out to renovate it or at least materials are being taken in and you can hear power tools being used. Then it's over to the marina to look into the water. There are a lot of small fish but also a lot of litter and we wonder whether it is ever dredged? At the far end is a mock up of a Venetian Gondola which looks a little unstable in the harbour area and so not sure how well it will cope with the wilds of the Black Sea.

Through the marina area and up the hill to the hotel to pick up our gear and sort a taxi over to the station. Our driver is

---

[167] It hasn't!

very chatty when he finds out what we have done over the past few weeks. Maybe we've inspired him to travel?[168]

The station is as busy as you would expect on a Friday afternoon with little space to stand, let alone sit, in the main entrance area. The ticket office is off to one side in a very small, cramped area with lots of people lined up in a semi-orderly fashion. We join separate ones in the hope of moving through much quicker, its 1.20pm and we are wanting tickets for the 2pm train. My fellow queuers are intrigued that I am more concerned with writing in my little book than the speed of the serving.

I reach the front and am told that there are no second class tickets left for this train. What about first class? As a Yorkshireman I ask the obvious question; "How much?" We walk away having purchased two first class tickets for a 200+ km journey for about £37. H wanders off to get some food for the journey while I shoulder both the rucsacs and head to the platform.

The train pulls in and, as always, there is a bun fight as many of the passengers want to get on first. Are they under the impression, like many, that the first on board gets to drive the train? Even to our untrained eyes we can see that the train is overbooked and so we expect someone to be in our seats.

We are not disappointed.

Into Wagon 2, First Class, and go to seats 23 & 25.

---

[168] This is always our hope.

"Excuse me, 23 and 25" I wave the tickets.
"No, Wagon 2" is his defence, obviously thinking we are in Wagon 1.
"Yes, Wagon 2" I say pointing to the wagon number on the ticket.

Defeated the chancer takes his time unplugging his phone, gathering his stuff and getting up. He then stands up in the aisle (with others) for the journey[169]. The stowage of the rucsacs causes the usual problems (inadequate shelving) and we push them under the seats, much to the annoyance of those standing in the aisles who have to shuffle around. Our fellow passengers help by putting there, smaller, bags in the overhead shelves rather than on the floor (which we have taken over). So we are in and, relatively, comfortable. Looking around the carriage it appears that the first class compartment is little different from second class only that there are less seats resulting in a wider aisle. What this means is that we have more people wedged in the aisles who seem to be hovering waiting for any empty seats to become obvious.

We are sitting opposite a young couple (in their early twenties) who have a young baby. H, of course, gets the questions in early and we find out that she is called Alicia and she is seven months old. Mum and dad look absolutely knackered so she offers to nurse her for a few minutes, the few minutes last about twenty until she starts to fall asleep

---

[169] Like many people on this train they only had second class tickets but tried to get into first class. Unlike many other European countries this practice is tolerated/ignored in Romania.

and then she is returned to her, now sorted and settled parents.

H browses through her photos to remind us what we have been doing over the past three weeks and we realise what a long strange journey its been. Like many of the people on the train we catch some sleep, when I wake up I realise that many of the standing passengers are now sitting on the floor of the carriage (some asleep!).

We arrive in Bucharest on time and there is the usual rush of people trying to get on the train, in fact if you have ever seen a film involving a cavalry charge you can probably visualise it. Of course this means that no one can get off and a, sort of, Mexican stand off is achieved. Through this apparent blockage two people stumble into our carriage as if shot through a gun – still no one has managed to get off! We shoulder our rucsacs and go to investigate the best way out, mainly out of concern that we may end up heading north towards Brasov.

At the door we see that common sense has started to prevail and people are managing to get off, although those commanding the step still appear to be trying to get on. We push through the chaos and H drops down onto the platform first, as I watch I notice that the way she carries her rucsac is helping her get through the crowd and adopt a similar technique with mine. This is, effectively, making sure that the rucsac keeps swaying from left to right as you move. Whilst most people do get out of the way those who don't get a knock from it. Maybe next time they will remember to move?

So, we are back in Bucharest. Of course the station is at the opposite end of the town from the hotel we are staying in. How to get there? H thinks that a taxi is too easy so we set off into the underground (knowing where we are heading does make this a lot easier).

The Bucharest Underground is best described as 'rock solid'. John, who we met on the ferry to the Delta, said it has two major flaws; firstly it does not go far enough in any direction and, secondly, it doesn't have enough stations. He is right on both accounts, still you can't have everything! Head for a machine to circumvent the problem we had last year (of trying to find a someone to buy a ticket from) and manage to purchase them. We now go to the platform, although this isn't without incident as we struggle to get the machine to work and a local has to point out that you have to put the ticket in upside down, "It's poor.....er.....er...." and waves his arms, "design?" I suggest, "da" comes the reply and we all laugh at the fact that putting a piece of tape over the arrow on the machine would solve the problem. To platform 3G stopping on the way to check the vague map. It lacks many stations that we know exist (they are on our detailed Bucharest map). Next to it is an electronic display that lists a few more stations. This helps a little but still some stations are not shown.

The train takes us straight through to Uniri then we wander around trying to get out. The signage is ok up to a point, that point being where one of the exits is closed off. Go the other way and by the time we reach the surface think that we would have been better walking all the way from the Gare de Nord!

Out onto the surface and fresh air. We quickly get our bearings as, looking down a very wide boulevard, we can clearly see the Palace of the People. Make a mental note that more of the fountains appear to be working than last time. From here it's easy to find the hotel as it's on the edge of the Old Town in a pedestrian zone (last year the taxi driver struggled to explain what a pedestrian zone was to us). We go to book in.

How times and staff change, last year we were greeted by a jolly group of staff on reception who were amused by the Newby Cat reference, found two English people of a certain age backpacking a little odd, were happy to chat with us and were interested in what we had been doing (or at least pretended to be). This year we're being served by the B team (possibly even lower)! The man on reception seems to be not bothered at all, in anything, and feels that booking us in is something of a chore (we even get a sigh as he is doing so). The bellboy, on the other hand, is full of enthusiasm and is waiting to load up our luggage with his little trolley.

"If you want breakfast then it's 10€" says Mr Happy behind the counter.
"Oh, I thought that breakfast we included?"
"No!"
"Are you sure?"
"Yes!!"

Now I know that according to what he has in front of him we hadn't booked breakfast but, clearly, we were under the impression that we had so a little customer service would have been nice[170], maybe just a small pause before saying no

We accept defeat and head for our room on the fourth floor. Our luggage takes the lift whilst we take the stairs. To get to our room from the top of the stairs we have to cross a bridge/balcony that looks straight down into the foyer, maybe we should have been warned 'If any customers suffer from vertigo....' I have certainly felt happier.

The room is smaller than we had last year but at least it has a bath that H decides to utilise (the tub appears to be a bit short and anyone over 5ft 10in would struggle). We then discover that the only towels we have are small ones and there are no robes[171]. Can this be the same hotel that so impressed us a year ago. On the plus side we have BBC World so we can catch up on the news.

Out we go for food and into the Old Town, an area that we got to know very well last year and we look forward to see what has changed (there was a lot of new building under construction last year). We are not disappointed! Over near the old Stock Exchange (now a craft and antiques market) is an almost finished new Hilton hotel[172]. Last year this was very large building that had been totally gutted and reduced to merely a façade.

We end up in a restaurant we have eaten at before with the remains of the monastery in the outside space at the rear. We ask if we can sit at the back, inside, so we have this view. The owner asks if we will sit at the front, we think this is because they are expecting a large party inside, either that or

[170] Last year wc had a free upgrade as well as excellent service but it appears that the hotel has started to slip a little since then.
[171] Told you that standards had dropped.
[172] We knew it was Hilton as there was a large sign announcing that fact.

they want an odd English couple in the window as an advert[173]
We oblige and study the menu. H orders the chicken whilst
I have the local sausages, both with polenta (of course). A
couple of beers and, well filled, we head out into the night so
H can have a cocktail (something she has been talking about
for a couple of days). End up at Jack's Bar (Strada Lipscani
45) where, after a lot of thought and deliberation, H decides
on a Tokyo Iced Tea. The barman comes over to take our
order and she orders a Long Island! I go for a Holstein
Weizen due to the total lack of local beers on offer.

Jazz plays down the road and the sound drifts into the bar,
"At least its not Romanian music" comments H referring the
Euro-Pop that we have been subjected to over the last few
weeks in every bar. Having been in relative isolation over
that time it is strange that we are now dropped in to the
middle of the nation's bustling capital.

A man walks passed carrying a large, insulated, box that says
"Chicken Stuff" on the back and we wonder what is in it (but
daren't ask!). As it's Friday night there are a lot of parties
out. It appears to be the Romanian way that when work
finishes everyone heads for the pub to celebrate the fact. H
is in her element doing some people watching and she
embarks on a running commentary on everything from the
totally unsuitable footwear of the women who are out trying
to walk along the cobbles (its hard enough in trainers so
how they manage it in five plus inch heels we will never
know) through to how hot they must be in the jackets they
are wearing.

---

[173] 'The food here is so good even the made English couple eat here!'
could be the strap line.

Out of the night a drunken man stumbles towards me mumbling about lots of things in a language I could not comprehend (it certainly didn't sound Romanian, maybe Portugese?).

"I'm very sorry", I say in my best *Gentleman Traveller* voice, "but I don't know what you are talking about!". There then follows a very long pause, the sort that you wait for someone to come round with refreshments during, whilst my newly found friend processes the information. The light bulb comes on in his mind as he realises that he doesn't understand me either and stumbles off into the night.

More people watching follows, including a group of girls who appear to have gone to the same stylist as they have near identical dresses on just a variation on the colour red. Thirty minutes later my drunken friend returns (clearly not remembering me, although this is not unusual). He starts talking at me again, slurring even more and still not making sense.

"Once more my friend I am sorry but I still have no idea what you are talking about. Do you want to discuss some short term investment opportunities perhaps?" I gaze at him and can almost hear the cogs turning. "How is your life going? I'm trying to write a book, how about you?" I hold up my diary, "Maybe my PA could touch bases and arrange.....". He's walked off by the time I mention my book so conclude he won't be pre-ordering it which is a shame as he may have enjoyed it[174].

---

[174] Especially as he gets a mention.

It's an odd thing with beggars (as this is what I think my drunken friend was) as to how you act. In many provincial towns there are signs saying not to give anything as it can lead to problems (violence where money is not handed over). I have always chosen to try and make conversation with them to put them off their guard before not giving them anything. Our research suggests that many of the ones in Bucharest are part of a larger network.

Across the road from where we are sitting is Club Taboo, a night club, which has a large screen outside showing what is going on inside. A great idea except for the fact that for most of the evening it is just showing an error message and when it is fixed it just shows a blurred picture of something.

We try and order a decaffeinated frappe but without any success so it's a fully caffeinated version we have before we set off to try and find the AirBnB we are staying in for the rest of the trip. On the way to the flat we have a disastrous discovery as we find that not only is last year's kebab shop closed but the pizza place, where we couldn't work out how to order, is still open[175].

The instructions for the apartment say to meet the owner near the shoe shop next to the Erotic Superstore – we remember this from last year as it was the place where people slept in the doorway. The Superstore now looks closed but we guess that the doorway to the left of the main entrance is the one that goes up to the apartments.

---

[175] The ordering system was so complicated that we gave up after about ten minutes of wandering around.

Head back to the hotel via the other side of the unfinished Hilton, work is carrying on through the floodlit night so we wonder if they are targeting the completion date which is approaching fast.

Catch the end of Die Another Day before turning in.

Saturday 26th August – Around 2am I go to the bathroom (its my age). As I do I see light coming through the gap in the curtains, looking through the gap I see that a party is in full swing at the bar opposite. Noise from it is very muted by the windows so I adjust the curtains to block out all the light and go back to bed. H has a similar situation two hours later when the party is still in full swing.

As we get up and start to pack we check outside and see that the party has finished and apart from a few people who are sitting on the benches outside (party survivors) the road is empty. After a brief discussion we decide not to have breakfast in the hotel (they lost that add on with their behaviour when we arrived). Quick shower and we head down to reception.

Admiring our rucsacs the young receptionist starts to restore faith in the hotel as he asks after what we are doing and extends a far better quality of service than we had had yesterday, "Are you going to the mountains?". We explain what we have done and his eyes light up. He asks after the cost of the trip as "Many people spend 2,000€ for one week (on accommodation)!" We get the map out and show him our route explaining that we have stayed in a mixture of hotels, huts and camping. As we leave the hotel we hope that we have given him something to think about (and save up for). Rucsacs safely stored on the left luggage trolley.

We resist the temptation to go straight across the road for breakfast, although we think about just going in and being noisy to see how many are recovering from last night. Head into the Old Town to see what else is available.

Outside the 'Non-Stop Booze' hut (to call it a shop would be overglamourising it and its closed?) is our drunken friend from last night, fast asleep on the step, his yellow baseball cap being lit up by the early morning sunlight.

End up at the Xclusive Bar and Grill (odd name?) for breakfast, coffee and some people watching (which it is a good place for). The breakfast consists of; two slices of thick fatty bacon, three large eggs, tomatoes and sheep's cheese, a wonderfully eclectic combination that seemed to have been something that the chef just 'threw together' from what he had. I try a Viennese Cappuccino, which is basically a cup of warm cream with a shot of coffee in it. It's alright but wouldn't be on my list of things that I 'must have again!'.

From here we again meander back past the site of the lovely kebab shop from 2016, which has been replaced by a rather minimalist book shop[176]. Crossing the road we visit what is, possibly[177], the oldest church in Bucharest. We have walked past it a few times but it has either been closed or a service has been on so it is nice to finally get in. As we leave a very

---

[176] Minimalist in that it, not only has few books but also is painted very white with sparse wall coverings.
[177] Many churches claim this title and it is difficult to find which one truly is the oldest.

smartly dressed gentleman walks in, pauses for a minute and then walks straight out. A couple of minutes later a large, well dressed, party arrive as if the first man was the advanced party. We head in the other direction back to the hotel to collect our rucsacs.

Opposite the Erotica Mall[178] is a very nice little café (New York Coffee) so we order a coffee and make ourselves comfortable hoping that our 'an old couple with two big rucsacs' description will mean that Claudia will find us. She phones us at a little after 1pm, just as I am about to go to look for her; she is only a minute away. Knowing the Romanian approach to time keeping we order another coffee although we are surprised when she arrives soon after.

Prior to Claudia's arrival I had pointed out a door that appeared to bisect the Mall suggesting that was where the entrance to the apartments might be. Of course that is where we go in!

When you enter many of these apartment buildings in the old Soviet Bloc you really do feel as if you have walked out of the Twenty First Century and onto the set of a Cold War thriller. The entrance area is cold, grey and gives the impression of being an abandoned shop front with a desk being the only furniture after the last occupant had to do a runner. On the plus side there is no chalk mark in the floor where the body has been.

---

[178] For all its bluster the Erotica Mall is quite a small affair taking up a shop unit that is probably only about 4 metres by 4 metres. The rest of the shop beneath the huge banner hoarding sells mobile phones.

Another apartment block and another small lift. The three of us wedge in and go up to the seventh floor, room 40. The corridors of the seventh floor look like someone has been murdered in them, more dark, long areas that scream Cold War. We expect seeing Harry Palmer walking towards us. The automatic hallway lights appear to be quite hesitant about coming on and we have to stand and wave to set off the sensors.

Opening the door to Room 40 we step from 1959 into 2017 and a lovely apartment with a balcony, parquet floor and a very well equipped kitchen. Even H is impressed. Having handed over the keys Claudia tells us that she must go as she is meeting someone. Unfortunately she asks what we have been doing so its thirty minutes later when she finally leave. Her parents live in the south of Romania and she says how wonderful that area is near the Bulgarian border so we make a mental note to go there some time.

H goes for a lie down, I fall asleep on the sofa whilst watching the television.

An hour or so later we decide its time to head off into town to complete what we thought was some unfinished business (or more accurately places that we didn't visit last time). First up is the Art Gallery where last year we only had an hour to look round both of the wings and only got round the religious section. We go first to the European section that we had missed totally and have a very leisurely walk around. As always the assistants eye us suspiciously as if we are going to steal something. Having completed the European section we do a quick tour of the rest of the Gallery, much of which we had seen last year, then head back outside.

Up and across Calea Victorei we visit the Headquarters of the Romanian Society of Architects. This odd building was the main offices of the Securitate[179], the Romanian State Police, at the time of Ceausescu. They, and the buildings around them, are extensively covered with bullet holes following the events of December 1989 – across the way is the balcony where Ceausescu made his final speech before being helicoptered off the roof. It is an odd area that we walk across, in front of what are now Government offices, where thousands had booed the President prior to his short lived escape. The car parking area is filled with Dacia cars, which appear to be the standard Government issue.

On the same square is the Memorial of Rebirth, a large marble pillar that reaches to the sky, which has been referred to as both 'an olive on a toothpick' and 'the potato of the revolution. The number of times it has been vandalised confirms that it is not to everyone's taste but this has been in the form of painting (including some red paint near the top that gives the impression that it is bleeding). However, what we didn't expect to see and what horrifies us (not a strong enough word) was the damage inflicted on it by some local skateboarders who are using it as a ramp (one was there as we approached but made his excuses and left as we approached). All of the bottom marble section has been broken. Imagine the Cenotaph in Whitehall, London being subjected to similar abuse and you have a comparison.

Still grumping to each other we head off to try and locate a supermarket soon finding ourselves in a small Carrefour.

---

[179] Worth looking up about them. Basically very bad people.

This results in two things; firstly, we hardly get anything and, secondly, we get grumpy with each other! We quickly leave and head to the bigger one where we manage to get everything we need. Sadly we leave by the wrong exit and get totally lost wasting time wandering in and out of a multi-storey car park.

Our original plan was to go for cocktails but by the time we have sorted ourselves out its 8.30 so we head back to the apartment for Bones on the TV and a picnic style tea. Sadly we have bought some cheese that is too salty and some houmous[180] that has no flavour. We still eat it.

Catch the end of Charlie's Angels before we turn in for the night.

Sunday 27th August – we have the air conditioning on overnight to try and keep the temperature reasonable and just about manage it as the summer evening/night temperatures soar. In order to not waste energy we have turned off the one in the living area, which means that when we go to the toilet we are hit with a wall of heat.

Across the road from us, on the side of a large shopping mall is a huge electronic advertising hoarding that runs videos throughout the day and lights up our room. We work out that it goes off around midnight and then starts up again around 7am so the light pollution isn't too bad.

H has a disturbed night sleep, being kept awake by the LED readout on the air conditioning unit. She solves the problem

---

[180] I know that you can spell it several ways.

by wrapping a scarf around her eyes giving the impression she is facing a firing squad! Upon inspecting the unit I discover that you can easily turn if off.

Breakfast is a selection of meats and cheese from last night (even the salty one) together with hard boiled eggs. Different bread from last night (which was a sort of onion bread) and is very filling. The filter coffee machine is pressed into service and produces an acceptable cup, although we now have a kettle so we can have tea which is much nicer.

Sunday morning Bucharest is quiet as we leave the apartment and head to the Natural History Museum. This involves a metro trip and so we head south in search of a station. This has the added bonus that we have to walk past a lot of clothes shops so H can have a nosey around, although she points out that, "Everything is in piles in the middle, hardly anything on hangers with sizes shown", I choose the easy option and stay outside keeping an eye out for my drunken mate from the other day (I don't see him).

Use up our last metro credit to get us over to Victory Square which, again, seems very quiet. In the middle of the road where there is normally a large traffic island, made up of cars, all there is is a table and a computer type chair (if gives the impression of a Monty Python sketch).

We cross the road to the museum where we are greeted by a rather sad looking model giraffe whose legs look like they have been glued together on numerous occasions and then reinforced using a lot of fibreglass. It also has a long cable holding it down (has it previously been stolen?). We go inside and pay 50RON for the two of us (including a photographic pass). The museum is very well laid out with arrows indicating a direction of travel through the building. After our visit to the Delta we are able to tie up a few loose ends such as it was a White Tailed Eagle we saw. We can also confirm that it was a lynx that we saw when we were in the woods. More worrying is the size of the brown bear in the museum. The photo that we took of 'our bear' print has my boot along side for scale and we compare this to estimate the size of the bear that we were in the vicinity of. We conclude that the one that we saw was a cub and that it was the parent that had left the print as it was compatible with the one in the museum (which is big!).

The collection is vast but it is unclear where it all comes from and we conclude that much of it was hunted and collected during the Communist era[181]. Some of the animals were stuffed some time ago looking at the state of them and the fur could do with a bit of a comb to cover the stitch marks. Many of the fish appear to be held together with thick layers of varnish and happy memories.

Out of the museum and we go in search of a coffee and a snack. End up with a coffee at Gran Bistro, which is just down from both Starbucks and McDonalds and is reasonably busy (but offers a much better décor than the other two!). It appears to be mainly set up for the fashionable people from the offices, which are scattered around. The air conditioning is very welcome and the, now old and battered, Bucharest street map is spread out on the table to plan where we are

[181] Ceausescu was famous for organising hunting parties, although he was not a good shot.

off to next. We are in an area where there are lots of things to see so head out into the heat towards the Museum of the Romanian Peasant (or something like that). Sadly its closed and when I say closed I mean very closed – the skips outside suggest that it is being refurbished, there are no signs suggesting how long this is to take and so we look at Plan B.

Plan B is a long walk and we head for the Zambaccian Art Gallery, which we find tucked away in the middle of a housing estate in an Arts and Craft style house. The staff look at us strangely, obviously not used to British people going around. Actually they may just be surprised that someone has found the place! We look through the visitor's book and find the closest to us are a couple from Ireland who were here a month ago.

This is a lovely little gallery that has grown out of a private collection that was left to trustees to administer. Each of the rooms is crammed with pictures of varying sizes as if they are trying to fill every inch of the walls with art. Best room? The toilet, which is a very large bathroom, complete with bath! It also has some art on display.

Leave and head towards Herăstrău Park, a much easier task on paper than it is in real life as we have to cross and re-cross roads in order to move forward. It also involves having to avoid fenced off roads (not sure why they have done this) and road works (scattered everywhere). Sadly by the time we reach the bike concession it is closing so we wander over to the nearest bar to seek solace there.

Having sat at a table for about ten minutes one of the bar staff comes over and puts a third chair up to us as if we are expecting a guest[182] and then walks off! We think that the owner is on the table next to us as several members of staff keep coming over to him. In the twenty minutes we are there he has at least four cigarettes, smoking them at such speed that he would probably have qualified for the Olympics (if it was a sport) and we are toping up on the nicotine through secondary smoking. Pedalling up to the bar

---

[182] We aren't.

is a man on a very nice looking cyclo-cross bike who appears so happy that he may have just won the Tour de France. So happy in fact that he doesn't even bother locking it up (having leaned it against the 'owners' table). He disappears into the bar (emerging seconds later with a pint!) and stands admiring the world. Its an odd bar but we like it and can even forgive them for playing Sinead O'Connor at full blast.

The lack of bikes means that our visit to the park is limited and, having finished our drinks and waved to our host who is rummaging through his man bag for another pack of cigarettes, we head south past the statue of General DeGaulle. Here we pause to take a photo but are stopped as someone has chosen to climb on it in order to light up (is it easier to light a cigarette on the top of a Twentieth Century Icon?). A wedding party arrives in a battered van, or at least the bride and groom do, followed closely by a photographer. He appears to have considerably more cameras than he does hands and they juggle around on his neck as if he is leaping from a helicopter in 'nam like Dennis Hopper in Apocalypse Now. After saying that he only appears to use one of them which he keeps waving above his head to stop the straps tangling. We leave them to it and head for the Metro to University Plaza.

Of course we head out of the wrong entrance and end up at the InterContinental Hotel, which is on the wrong side of the busiest road in Bucharest. So it's a turn around and back underneath to relocate ourselves, admiring some of the graffiti on the way. On the plus side this means that H can try on a couple of outfits in an ethically produced shop which includes a dress that is big enough for not only H and me but also for most of the Household Cavalry. The owner is very positive and says is should be worn loose, I resist the temptation to say that it would be loose with a garage inside it.

Abandon the idea of wandering back to the apartment as H declares "I quite fancy a cocktail…" and we head towards Jack's. On our way we stumble across another shop where H decides to buy a shirt. After we have spent a considerable time trying to work out the sizing we are approached by an assistant who points out that "one size fits all" – a whole shop where sizing is not necessary, how weird is that. Whilst H does find a shirt she likes many others are rejected for the following reason, "one size doesn't fit anyone!"

Purchase made we arrive at Jack's so H can have her Tokyo Ice Tea and I make a note to look up what's in it as it takes a long time to arrive, my (unfiltered and so a little chewy) beer arrives straight away. In the background we can hear a man playing Hey Jude on what we think is a bow on a saw, it sounds odd and the waiter (who has a great moustache) points to his ear, then in the direction of the sound and says "tis creepy". As I struggle sifting the bits from my beer through my teeth we decide that food is required and, as Jack's menu is limited (and we fancy a kebab) head off towards the centre of the Old Town.

Manage to find a kebab shop only to discover that it is an, 'order here, pay here and collect over there' establishment. The main area, where you order, resembles the Stock Market in the old days with people waving their arms a lot showing pieces of paper as if they are trying to see dodgy stock! H walks off (she doesn't do queuing) and I am left trying to second guess how the system works. I adopt my best Alan

Whicker persona and bluff it through, walking to the counter ignoring anyone who is waving. H wants a chicken kebab whilst I fancy the adventure (and uncertainty) of a mixed one which may contain anything! They arrive with a small portion of rather disappointing chips and a can of Sprite. As I head out of the café I notice a sign declaring, "No bikes, no cats, no dogs, no alcohol" so we are happy with our drinks. The kebabs are very well packed and the sauce which they are served with is totally different from those in the UK, whether they are better is subject to debate. Park ourselves on the chairs that are in a fenced off area on the pavement.

Fed and watered (Sprited!) we head back towards the apartment via a couple of souvenir shops and try and decide what we are getting people[183]. H also finds a small building that matches the one she got last year and so decides she should have a small village on the mantelpiece at home.

Of course we are drawn back towards Jack's for a nightcap only to find ourselves walking past the source of the strange (creepy) noise from earlier. It is not a bow being drawn across a saw but some sort of strange noise generating machine that is being played by disturbing the sound waves[184]. Its very odd and we seek more information from the moustachioed waiter. He tells us that the 'musician' (he pauses whilst using the word) has invented it and it responds to his body movements, he waves his arms around. He pauses again, "Eet is very clever.....but I wish that he would go away!", one of the shops we have been in echoed

---

[183] As we have had to carry everything over the length of the trip we have been very wary about buying anything and so presents have been put on the back burner.
[184] Further research suggests that it is a sort of theremin.

that view asking that we close the door to keep the 'noise' out. In Bucharest everyone is a critic.

As we watch the world go by a woman walks by who appears to be dressed as Arthur Dent from Hitchhiker's Guide to the Galaxy wearing a red plaid dressing gown. As she gets closer we think that it may be a wraparound dress, although it does look very much like a gown!

Our location is perfect for people watching as it is at the meeting of three of the busiest roads in the district but this also means that acoustically it is quite challenging. Above the sound of the crowds we have the 'saw man', a violinist and a jazz bar up one road, a solo accordionist up another and finally a boom box (which is getting progressively louder) up a third.

Each bar has someone who has the job of encouraging people to come up and we get chatting to the one at Jack's after we comment that she is yawning at 9pm. She has another six hours before she finishes her shift. The bar serves food from 10am until 2.30am but we get the impression that it is open the rest of the time for drinks. Amongst the food on offer is 'Jack's All Day Breakfast' and 'Jack's in the UK' but we don't try either of them.

The TV in the corner is switched over to football and the volume cranked up to dominate the area. This leads directly to us being joined, on the next table, by a soccer mad group of lads who stack their table with packs of cigarettes and set about working through them. H shuffles her chair around to reduce the risk of secondary smoking. The game is FCSB vs

FCB[185], and whilst it seems popular in the bars the stands at the stadium look quite empty.

As the people watching continues we are brought a tray of nibbles (gratis) by one of the bar staff who appears to have put a value on having a middle aged English couple sitting outside of the bar. Our next sight is that of a heavily bandaged person in a wheelchair being brought past us as if they have been sprung from hospital in order for them to go for a beer!

With our nicotine levels nicely topped up we leave our football friends to carry on shouting at the match and meander back to the apartment where we find we have received an email from Booking.com asking for our comments on the last hotel. I feel bad about writing a poor review.

Monday 28th August – We are awake at 7am after a terrible night's sleep (we blame the alcohol). H stumbles into the shower whilst I do the coffee wrestle as I try to get a cup out of the machine. Kettle boiling separately means that tea is also supplied. Breakfast is what we find in the fridge whilst watching a William Holden war film.

Suitably fortified we remember to pick up our IDs and head out in search of bikes. As we are going south we need to find the right underground station and head towards Unirii 2 for the blue line. One stop and we are at Tineretului (yes, H bought a dress on the way). We came here last year on the

[185] FCSB is Fotbal Club Steaua Bucureşti and FCB is Futbol Club Barcelona

recommendation of the apartment owner and having been told of a wildlife area beyond it we feel that it is worth a visit Bikes are the ideal way to explore.

The bikes are 5RON per hour so we go with three hours and set off. Immediately I am surprised by the noise coming from my bike. Its surprising as its not making a noise; no grating or clunking. We climb up through the park pausing at the bridge where, last year, we saw a three way standoff between terrapins, ducks and fish! This year they seem much happier as a man turns up and starts throwing large pieces of bread to them which the fish devour as if they are pyranhas. The ducks and terrapins take a back seat and pick up any pieces that drift their way. H points out that you shouldn't feed them bread but they take no notice.

Still heading south we go around the large sports hall (all refurbished since last year) and find ourselves in another park with lots of children's rides in it. Now in a new area we park up near a water fountain that people appear to be making a pilgrimage to in order to fill their water containers which come in all shapes and sizes. Cars are queuing up on the approach road and so we join the queue. Water bottles filled we head out of the park into a housing estate, using a large transmitter tower as a reference point to take us towards the Parcul Natural Văcărești. We zig-zag through the estate having to remind ourselves to keep to the right as the cars aren't really observing the rules of the road[186].

By going with this route we are disgorged onto a, very, main road and see Sun Plaza, a large out of town shopping centre

---

[186] They just drive where there are less pot holes.

at the top of a steep hill. According to Google Maps this is on the edge of the park and, after a little scouting around, we find a service road that takes us past it towards our goal. Unfortunately on our left there is an extremely high fence that blocks a direct way through and so we push on in the hope of finding a gate at the corner (Google suggests a path exists there).

At the corner there is no gate. On the plus side there is no fence! A section of it has, almost surgically, been removed (making us wonder what the purpose of it was in the first place). We dismount and tentatively wheel our bikes through the overgrown bushes and then pause as we take in the view.

We are standing on the edge of a huge tract of wasteland, that goes as far as the eye can see. To our left and right, on each side, there are large blocks of flats (concrete of course) but in the middle there is an area covering many acres[187]

that appears to have been prepared ready to make a large reservoir but then abandoned as Communism collapsed. It is now an almost post-apocalyptic area where you expect dinosaurs to now flourish. What is clear is that it is a very odd area! As we stand there trying to work out if we can cycle around it we are approach by a man who seems to have appeared out of nowhere;

"Excuse me", he says in near perfect English, how did he know that we were English? Maybe only English people stand here staring out at the wasteland taking pictures.
"Er, yes", I reply, resisting the temptation to ask how he got here or how he knew we were English.
"Would you like a bible?" It seems a very odd question to be asked but he is very polite.
"No thank you", beyond anything else there was the weight issue, it looked a big, well bound, copy.
"Okay, do you believe in Jesus Christ?" he didn't specify any context so I felt happy to reply yes. He just smiled, turned and walked away. The next time I looked he had gone, where I couldn't guess but he appeared to have covered a great distance in a very short space of time.

Whilst I was having this strange encounter H has walked a section of the track and declares it bikeable. We look down into the 'bowl' and see a couple of people who are walking towards the forested area in the middle along what looks like a prepared track. We cycle along the rim of the area, below us the sides resemble the steepness of a giant velodrome. Sadly we also witness that, in many places, it has been used as something of a dumping ground as the slopes

---

[187] Over 400 acres.

are strewn with all sorts of rubbish. We pedal on staying on the edge of the area as we think to venture in would require more substantial footwear than the sandals that we are wearing.

Suddenly we hear dogs, lots of dogs and H thinks that they may be in a pack and comments as such. Then they appear, about a dozen of them running up from a 'gypsy' village which has been established on the edge of the park. They are very barky and appear to know where the gap in the fence is as they chase after the pair of us. H is at the front and so the lead dog comes after me. I am very conscious that it may be me or him and so adjust myself accordingly expecting my wheels to make contact. The dog appears to realise this and so, having seen me off what they see as their patch they back off. Around the corner H is waiting for me. Here the path becomes very well maintained and, more strangely, signs start to appear telling us how far it is to go round etc. (even though the section we have come along was overgrown). Beyond the first set of signs there are some steps that go down into the 'trench' with some matting and a hand rail to help (although part of me wonders if this is just there to stop people wandering off the main path and falling down!). I duck underneath the rope that blocks the slopes off to get a better photograph whilst H heads off to check the route away from the park. Thanks to the clear signage we soon find ourselves descending near Asmati Gardens (these aren't gardens at all but large flats) and heading back to the city. We then try and find our way back to the Tineretului via a lower path to take the bikes back. This involves a few near misses with cars, H almost taking out a couple of people who decide to walk out in front of her and a glider that is placed on a lawned area as if it has flown in this morning.

There is no plaque saying why it is there but we conclude that it is in memory of someone.

Bikes returned only just outside our time and we head for the nearest cafe for a frappe as the rain clouds start to gather. As we sit the café owner starts to pull down the roof sections over the frame to keep the tables dry (keeping customers dry is just a bonus). Ignoring the gathering of the storm clouds we set off in the direction of Parcul Carol, which we had been close to last year, and the Memorial to the Fallen[188]. Without the bikes we are able to get much closer than previously although fences around the main part (and the presence of armed guards) mean that any closer inspection is limited. The bench, where last year we had leaned the bikes, has a very pleasant lady sitting on it who is watching the world go by and knitting at such speed that a jumper is almost formed in the time we wander around.

We walk down the steps in front of the memorial, which traditionally is used by runners as a training route but there are none today.   Then to the extensive ponds to look at the rather large fish. As this would be a very inconvenient time for the rain to start then this is what happens, we have no waterproofs or umbrella. The fish take the best option and descend. We seek shelter in an abandoned wooden ice cream kiosk together with a grandma and her grandchildren In the traditional way we smile and acknowledge each other but say nothing as the rain gets heavier. Then the storm hits complete with thunder and lightning and lots and lots of

---

[188] The name during the Communist regime was "Monument of the Heroes for the Freedom of the People and of the Motherland, for Socialism" which I think we can safely say is quite an impressive name.
.

rain! I suggest that it will be over in 15 minutes and we watch the area around us slowly flood. In the middle of the deluge a young couple, who are soaked through, stop on the path and kiss. Very romantic, but very wet.

After about ten minutes our fellow kiosk dwellers decide to make a break for it despite the rain not letting up. Five minutes later the rain stops as quickly as it had started. The air is clear and whilst it does feel a little cooler it is much more comfortable than it was 'pre-storm'. The local sparrows, who have been sheltering in the trees, swoop down and bath in the newly formed pools whilst the ducks start quacking like crazy and splashing around (scaring the sparrows).

From here it's an easy walk through the back streets to the Old Town once more passing the People's Palace where I take a few time lapse videos that will probably never see the light of day[189]. As we try and cross one of the roads a cyclist with a large box on the pannier carrier almost knocks H over (her fault), she has a laugh with the rider about her incompetence and asks, "What's in the box?" with no reply forthcoming she follows up with "Is there a body in there?". The lad smiles nicely and pedals off, only to reappear a few minutes later holding onto the back of another cyclist being towed along.

Decide to try our luck at getting a table in the Caru' cu bere[190] for dinner, although as we have not booked we don't hold

[189] Its not that they are rubbish, its just that in the modern age with digital photographs it appears that everyone takes twenty times as many pictures as they will ever watch.
[190] Caru' cu bere is a Bucharest institution which has been around for

our breath. Yes, they have a table but it is in the downstairs section of the restaurant (which means the cellar and we won't get the floor show, fair enough as we've seen it before). So down the stairs we go to share a knuckle of pork. Another English couple arrive prompting H to say, "They want to gather all the English people together down here so its easier to serve tea!" After a brief exchange they head off to the other side of the room and further into the bowels of the establishment. Behind us is possibly the largest and most Heath Robinson style first extinguisher I have ever seen. It is a 'normal' shape but scaled up with a pump on top to pressurise it, has large Keystone Cops type wheels and a large handle by which to tow/drag it.

The rain, that had abated has started again in earnest as we leave the Beer Wagon[191] and we shelter underneath the outside canopy (much to the amusement of the outside diners). Here we try and work out where we need to be and can we stay dry getting there. After a little thought we decided to head off to the Old Stock Exchange which is now a large craft area (the main hall has been closed on each of our recent visits so we have only been able to get into the foyer area). Despite our best efforts, of dodging in and out of shop doorways, we are soaked by the time we reach it only to find that the main hall is still closed. We make do with a mooch around the stalls by the foyer before heading off towards Jack's for one last visit taking in one of the standard issue souvenir on the way. The sympathy of the staff is delightful towards the two clearly deranged and bedraggled English couple...... who stumble in. We are offered paper towels to

---

130 years.
[191] The literal translation of Caru Cu Bere

try and dry ourselves off. Once more we are impressed by the kindness of strangers, although we really need bigger/more towels. We buy a small Roman statuette that is not dissimilar to The Thinker for 100RON (which is 30RON less than we have seen them elsewhere[192]).

We reach Jack's to find our friend is wrapped in a blanket still trying to get people in despite the fact that there is hardly anyone about. As all of the outside tables and chairs are either stacked (to keep them dry) or soaked we head inside where it is, unexpectedly, busy. I am told that I cannot have a beer as it is our last night and all that, so instead opt for a Hurricane cocktail which seems to be rum with added rum and some mango served is a vase type glass. It looks very orange. When it is brought to the table H comments to the waiter that it's not really a man's drink, to which he suggests that I might want a beer! H orders a Blue Lagoon which lives up to its name as its very, very blue. Its blueness reminds me of the colour of the effluent pond that you can see near the end of the Three Peaks of Yorkshire.

It's still relatively early and still raining as we head back to the apartment. Tomorrow is going to be a long day's travel so an early night is required and we hope that the rain will stop. Elementary, the US version of Sherlock, is on. It's rubbish.

Tuesday 29th August – time to head home. I am up at about 8am and start packing whilst H, who has had a rather disturbed night's sleep, slumbers on for another hour or so. We have until 11am to be out so have plenty of time. Finally

---

[192] We later spot them for 80RON

decide to wake her up with coffee at 9am. Actually what I do is creep in and leave the coffee on the side then, having retired to a safe distance, tell her that there is coffee (never wake a slumbering H). A grunt is uttered, she rolls over and goes back to sleep.

A quick check of the food supplies and I find that we have;
  2 eggs (boiled)
  An apple
  2 ROM bars
  2 cans of Ursus

We decide that we will leave the cans for the next residents, the rest will be consumed as we pack and then we can head out and get some breakfast whilst out and about.

9.30 and H is looking more awake as she complains about the taste of the coffee (the filter machine is not the best we have encountered). Propped up she reads her Kindle before showing very little interest in packing.

As 11 approaches I balance the camera on a shelf to take a self portrait of the pair of us. Then, at 11am on the dot the door bell rings, it's the cleaner. This we take as our indication to leave, shoulder our packs and make our way down the stairs.

The heavy downpour that had continued through the night has, fortunately, blown itself out although the drains have not coped well and there is a considerable amount of standing water. As we leave we notice that the Erotica Mall is closed until 2nd September, the mobile phone shop at the other side of the door is open and very busy.

We walk back up the main road so H can have a look at some of the clothes. She immediately comments that she should have been here three weeks ago so she could get something for travelling in. Of course she didn't buy anything this time around.

Time to try and find somewhere for breakfast. Our initial thoughts are to go to a place opposite the Europa Hotel until we realise that it is just an outfitters that also sells sandwiches and drinks. Around the corner is a Lebanese restaurant that is open and, whilst it's almost lunch time, feel that it is suitable for a late breakfast. A lovely platter to share between the two of us with numerous different types of meat and a rather pleasant aubergine mash (a little like humous) is brought out. For the next twenty minutes we are the only people in the restaurant. Our main company is in the form of a, very, pregnant cat which is wandering around. Once the crowds start to arrive, as they do in their droves then the restaurant quickly fills up.

The sun comes out a little after noon and with it the street slowly comes to life. From our comfy position we watch as groups of people come through almost in pulses of between ten and fifteen followed by a gap of a couple of minutes, then another group. It's as if around the corner there is a minibus drop off point that is ferrying people in[193]. A heavy police presence is also obvious, including a few heavily armed ones in full riot gear (why, we are not sure).

---

[193] There isn't, I checked

Finish our Lebanese breakfast (not sure if it was meant to be breakfast but it worked for us) and conclude that it should see us through to the airport later this afternoon and set off for some souvenir shopping. Almost immediately we find ourselves in the middle of a very well organised walking tour where the leader has a radio microphone and all the tourists have little headsets on with a radio receiver around their necks. They are all walking in step as if it's an army unit on manoeuvres, but with less khaki or flags.

We peel off and walk past the police station where one of the admin staff has stepped outside for a cigarette. She leans on the, now parked and propped up, Segway that we had seen an officer charging around on yesterday. Presumably the Robocops aren't out on patrol today! Down under our usual underpass to the Intercontinental Hotel where there is, as always, a long queue of grumpy looking taxi drivers who appear to be avoiding people who may want to get a lift to somewhere, anywhere. We approach the first taxi, "Airport?", and without question the boot is popped open, the driver gets out and our gear is stowed. Not sure that this has ever happened before. Unfortunately there are blinds or the windows of the taxi so photographs/videos are not possible which is a shame as we pass the Arc de Triumphe which is finally free from any hoardings or fencing. In fact it looks surprisingly good and we regret not walking out to it on Sunday when we were in the Park.

Dropped off, cost 25RON, we thank the driver and give him 30. Last time here we had made the driver promise to look after the country until we returned but at this time we are not sure when we will return so don't ask for the same commitment.

So we are back in the airport with plenty of time to kill before our flight. The arrivals/departures boards in the entrance area only show limited information and it takes us a few minutes to remember that we have to go and hunt down the relevant small screens to find out where we go from. H goes to a snack machine and somehow get a free Fagaras bar.

Parcel up the rucsacs and book the body bags in before wandering through to Passport Control where a nice little queue is moving much more briskly than we are used to. The security x-ray for my bag highlights the drybag that is full of charging wires and battery packs which the staff find quite amusing, especially when I have a moan with the line "well, if manufacturers do insist on different connectors....". A quick check reveals that there is nothing of concern and I am waved through with a friendly smile. The friendliness may also have been provoked by me mocking my eyesight without my glasses on and having to feel my way through the metal detector – it must be a rather tedious job so a smile obviously goes a long way.

Through to the Duty Free area where H discovers what we have thought for some time and that is that it's not as cheap as it used to be. This is made more entertaining by us being able to check the price of many of the gins on the Morrisons[194] website! What we also discover is that they do not take RON so it looks as if we will be going home with a week's worth of currency.

---

[194] Other supermarkets are available.

Find where our flight is going from and sit down. There is a queue but the gate isn't open yet so what's the point of wasting energy by standing up. Ten minutes later the flight is called and lots of people rush to the gate. Once more I ponder whether they think that they can fly the plane if they are first one on board – we all have reserved seats so why do people do this? Wait until the bun fight is over and then join the back of the queue. As we walk onto the plane we spot our seats, they are the only empty ones left on board. I suddenly have a crazy idea, what about letting people on a row at a time[195]?

In front of us is a small child, aged six or seven, with an iPad. To pass the time he is playing a nice gentle blasting game that seems to involve more kills than a Rambo film, and certainly a lot more blood. As the safety procedure is explained one of the passengers tries to go to the toilet but is told, in no uncertain words, to sit down. Then proceeds to make a play for the overhead lockers but again is told no.

We manoeuvre away from the terminal and the pilot, who had previously been waving at us when we were boarding, informs us that we have missed our take off slot but still hopes to get us into Amsterdam on time. The sister of the 'killing game' child is also blasting away on a game that appears to be based around Dunkirk.

So, once more, we bid farewell to Romania.

It's a packed a flight as we expected but the cabin crew are on top form and the food (penne pasta arrabbiata) is

---

[195] Another email that isn't sent.

immediately rolled out. Beer or wine is offered but its water for us as we try to rehydrate. Cutlery (plastic) is given out in neat little rolls that double as place mats, this seems quite an odd idea but does make the plane look very neat. Grab a post-pasta thirty minute nap although the last thing I see before drifting off and the first thing I see after waking up is the same view of the iPad blasting away (he obviously has the unlimited bullets option). Nice piece of lemon sponge (small, economy size) is served.

I head off to the toilet and, whilst waiting get to have a glance around the galley. What a well organised (small) area this is, lots of lists posted everywhere and then I spot them – the asbestos gloves. Wonder if these are for when the food comes out of the oven?[196]

We approach Amsterdam in thick cloud so we miss out on the usual views over the dykes and canals that we have become used to. Land and taxi into position. As expected even before the seatbelt light goes off, and whilst we are still moving, people are trying to stand up and get to their gear from the overhead lockers. They stand with their hands on the locker handle and wait, and wait. Ten minutes pass before they can open the lockers and start to disembark. We have spent that time reading. In no rush we are not the last to get off but close. Walking through the terminal we start chatting to a Romanian girl who is heading to Manchester to study Computer Science at the University and help each other find gate D16 where we will depart from. More price comparison at the Duty Free where a bottle of gin that costs

---

[196] Another Cabin Pressure reference.

€44 here can be bought for £35 at home. As the Euro/Sterling rate is close to parity then we put it back.

Tempted, once again, by the large Toblerone and the limited edition Miffy but we leave having only bought an inflatable plane and some biscuits. A screaming child in the shop breaks up the atmosphere and we compare notes on parenting with the cashier who, being Dutch, speaks excellent English.

Head back to D16 where the queue appears to disappear into the far horizon and sit down towards the front of it. Let the queue come to us, which it eventually does. Once more we join the queue of self loading human freight. As we join we hear the voices of two English businessmen who are returning home and we have a lovely chat with them about nothing in particular. H points out that this is the first long chat we have had with any English people (apart from each other) in four weeks.

We make the short hop to Manchester with no issue, it's the usual take off – food served – plane lands routine that we have done before. In fact the only difference appears to be the good weather over the UK so we get to see the lights of the major cities below us with H trying to work out which is which. Crossing the Pennines we know we are almost home.

The landing is nowhere near as dramatic as the one in 2016 when it was aborted and we had to go around for another lap. It's also a smooth transition through the arrivals area, which is relatively quiet. Body bags retrieved and we head for the outside to find our lift home. The taxi driver phones to say that he was in the main car park and was going to come around to pick us up. He appears a few minutes later and we are whisked back across the Pennines with him wanting to know all about the adventures we have had. We are more interested in what has happened back in the UK.

Our gateless drive greets us back home[197], the keys (stored in its usual place in the top of H's rucsac) is retrieved and in we go.

All trips of this nature end in a very similar way; you get back, you are safe and all you want to do is climb into bed and hope that the laundry pixies wash and sort all of your gear whilst you are asleep. So this is how this adventure draws to a close. We make an effort, of sorts, to unpack but this mainly just involves half emptying the rucsacs onto the dining room floor and put the pan set in the sink.

It is always the case that the only people who can understand a trip like this are those who have done something similar and the only people who can fully understand are those who are there. Our conversation as we rummage through our gear turns to what we could have left behind, I suppose the tent was always something of a wild card and the fact we only used it for one night does make us wonder, but the full kit post mortem will have to wait for another day.

Time for bed.

---

[197] See the first book. A friend of ours was restoring it for us but it still hadn't come back.

Travel Tips

The following are some tips that we put together on our travels that will mean that the trip will float by 'on gilded wings'. There is no science behind them or technical research.

1.   Remember what Hemingway said, "Never go on trips with anyone you do not love". It is unlikely that a ropey relationship will be saved by some close quarters travelling and we have seen several couples whose relationships were put under extreme pressure when a train broke down etc. Make sure that any travel companion is tolerant of your foibles, and you of theirs.

2.   Don't expect the unexpected and try and plan for it. When it happens, you won't expect it to happen again and won't be expecting it! (You may need to read that sentence again).

3.   Wet wipes and anti-bacterial gel can make travel much more pleasant and hygienic. I have been told that you can start a fire using some gels like a fire lighter but have never tried it.

4.   Try and sample the local food. Its very easy to slip into the "I'll have pizza" mentality and go on about how

much nicer the ones are from Dominoes 'back home'. To experience a country you must experience the food.

5.   Drink what the locals have. Don't go into a bar in Slovenia, Romania or for that matter Wasdale and ask for a pint of Stella! Order the local beer if you drink beer or local wine if that's your tipple. Try lemonade with mint/strawberry/ginger, you'd be surprised how nice it is. After saying all that then be careful of the locally stilled moonshine.

6.   Talk to the locals. Most are happy to suggest places to go. Some you may ask will look wistfully into the middle distance as you have stirred happy memories and made their day by asking their opinions. Others will say places where they would go if they had the chance and are willing you to live their dreams.

7.   Use local transport. Not necessarily all the time but certainly for most of it. If you are in a car then you are in a bubble and all you see are the roads. Trains and buses are great to see (experience) a country, if you use the underground then even better.

8.   Don't take the kitchen sink with you, you don't need to take it. Think carefully about everything that you take. If you are going to eat out all the time then check the dress code for the country and take the minimum. Can you wash clothes as you travel around (don't take dry clean only stuff)

9.   Take your own sink plug. One of those multisize ones like one from TrekMates. That way you won't find yourself stuffing toilet paper into the plug hole. Assume that for whatever reason there will be no plugs in sinks or showers.

10.   Ask people who have been before for advice, especially about the culture of a country. This advice comes with two caveats; firstly ignore the advice of anyone who went all inclusive and secondly ignore anyone who says "Oh, you must eat at...." or even worse, "go to <insert bar name here> and talk to Luigi, if you mention my name you will get great service". Unless of course the giver of the advice is a travel or food writer.....or Ernest Hemingway.

11.   To start a conversation, with a fellow traveller, on a train say "Are you going to...." Having previously check where the train terminates. Showing interest in where they are heading will usually get a positive response.

12.   Whilst we would never suggest that you abandon your own personality you should respect local customs and their ways. If you want to get drunk, shout a lot and be generally rowdy then stay at home and trash your own house. You are a visitor and respect that fact.

13.   Buy a note book. You don't have to keep a diary (God forbid) but you will scribbled notes that will remind of the trip. No matter how hard you try you will forget. This also

helps with arguments that happen years later about where/when you saw/did something. This together with the thousands of photos you take guarantee that you will bore everyone you meet. You could also produce a book.

14.   I am very poor at learning languages but always try and learn a few words such as 'hello', 'please' and 'thank you'. Think how much better people will treat you if you have made the effort to learn their language rather than just shouting "Oi Dave, two beers please!". H has always recommended learning "Do you understand English" in preference to "Do you speak English" as when people realise that you have tried to learn a little will try and speak back. Similarly if you aren't sure how to pronounce a place name then give it a go whilst showing them the map/app. Then have a laugh together as they correct you.

15.   Common sense says that you should not only obey the laws of the land but also respect local customs, so try and find out what they are. Nothing is more annoying than hearing someone say "Oh! I don't agree with that" or "What a stupid law!" then proceeding to drive off at high speed with no lights on.

Sadly I do not know who said this but its very similar to what H always says about remembering what went wrong on a trip;

"It is not the destination where you end up but the mishaps and memories you create along the way."

Happy travels my friends.

Gary & Helen Bacon

About the Authors

Gary Bacon is a teacher and trainee Gentleman Traveller. Through Scouting he developed a love for travel and canoed in Canada, spent six weeks in the Himalayas and been climbing in the Alps on numerous occasions. He shocked everyone in 2016 by being appointed an ambassador for the Original Mountain Marathon. He should train for the runs he does but keeps putting it off.

Helen Bacon works in education at an important level after many years as a classroom teacher. Amongst her many achievements are; she was the fastest woman in a 27 mile fell race, has flown various winged aircraft, taken part in endurance mountain bike races and mountain marathons. Her other hobbies include; trying to teach her husband about different leaves on trees and trying to find the perfect cocktail. She can proficiently gut a fish.

Over their 30 years of marriage they have travelled extensively throughout the UK and Europe on foot, by car and public transport. They can normally be found watching the world go by, and the rain fall, from a small tent. They no longer have any pets and wish that certain broadband providers would stop writing to them.

"An old couple with two big rucksacks" on the move again. This time with added bears, lynx and Polish people.

St 4

Helen at Parcul Natural V

Printed in Poland
by Amazon Fulfillment
Poland Sp. z o.o., Wrocław

54059875R00171